DOCUMENTS
ON THE MEXICAN REVOLUTION

Volume V

OTHER VOLUMES IN THIS SERIES

BLOOD BELOW THE BORDER

American Eye-witness Accounts of the Mexican Revolution

Edited & Introduced

by

Gene Z. Hanrahan

DOCUMENTARY PUBLICATIONS

Salisbury, North Carolina, U.S.A.

1982

INTRODUCTION

    This collection consists of twenty reports, letters and documents written by Americans in Mexico during the first years of the Mexican Revolution. None of these writings was intended for publication. In a majority of cases, they represented confidential reports directed to American officials and congressmen, designed to provide these leaders with what the authors believed was a true picture of history as it was happening. None of the writers feared open publication; none feared embarrassment or libel. So they wrote with a refreshing freedom seldom found in the works of professional writers. Furthermore, we find throughout scattered records of conversation with key Mexicans during the Revolution, a number of which cast interesting light on otherwise confusing events of the era.

The authors included here are as diverse as their writings. Many were Americans in business, their backgrounds reflecting long years of life and work in Mexico. Other writers were diplomats, visiting statesmen or mine managers. Significantly, in almost every case, they understood as well as any American can, the Mexican people and their politics. This is not to suggest that these authors were without prejudice. Throughout this book one senses the writers' basic concerns about the future of Americans in Mexico, and most particularly their concerns about the safety of American lives, investments and money. Some of the authors held for the maintenance of the status quo, thereby ensuring their financial and job security; yet a surprising number saw the exploitation of the peon, sensing the winds of change more accurately than many contemporary Mexicans, and honestly suggesting American policies towards the Revolution and its leaders which would not necessarily accrue to long run United States business and commercial interests in that nation.

This volume of Documents on the Mexican Revolution represents a departure from those previously published. Earlier volumes concentrated either on specific time periods or events. This volume, and the succeeding one, cover a longer, more amorphous spectrum of both time and events. Still the editor believes the inclusion of such volumes at this juncture serves an important purpose. That purpose rests in providing the reader with an emotional, pictorial feel for this violent era which might be lost in reading solely from the offtimes dry diplomatic correspondence which has been the mainstay of earlier volumes. No less important is the need here to infuse this collection with the observations and plight of Americans caught up in one violent moment of Mexican political history. Only in that way can the serious reader understand how Americans from various walks of life saw and understood what was happening, and how their reports and views helped shape United States policy towards that land and its chaotic political history.

As with all other documents in this series, these materials are a true record from original writings deposited in the United States National Archives in Washington, D.C. In keeping with the format of earlier volumes, no significant alterations have been made to either the substance or format of the materials included here.

Gene Z. Hanrahan

* * * * * * *

C O N T E N T S

MEXICAN MILITARY LEADERS

General V. Carranza

Pancho Villa

The Zapata Brothers and an American Soldier
in Vera Cruz, 1914.

Black American Soldiers captured in Carrizal
and returned through El Paso.

Villa and General Pershing one year before
the attack on Columbus.

Emiliano Zapata
and his
Anglo mistress
Margaret Benton
(Maggie Murphy).

Villa's "American Legion" outside Juarez, 1911.

An unidentified wounded American
about to be executed in Parral.

Washington,
March 31, 1911

E. M. Hood

You will find herewith an account of the conference on Sunday March 26th, attended by Senor de la Barra, Dr. Gomez and myself. I have prefaced it with a memorandum of certain details of the New York conferences, attended by Limantour, the Maderos and Gomez, which, to my knowledge never have been correctly stated.

David Lawrence.

New York Conferences

Limantour has made several evasive denials and has at the same time bound the Maderos and Dr. Gomez to secrecy. The facts are these:

Four conferences were held. In the first two conferences, Limantour, Dr. Gomez, Francisco Madero Sr., and Gustavo A. Madero, made excellent progress. In the third conference, I am informed by Gomez, Limantour showed almost a complete change. The conference ended in a disagreement, Gomez leaving in a huff. That night (the eve of Limantour's departure), the two Maderos prevailed upon Gomez to reduce to writing the tentative basis by which peace might be arranged. The Maderos took this to Limantour; Gomez did not see Limantour again. The Maderos reported that he had taken the proposals and had promised "a complete change" in the government. Limantour during this time received some kind of a message from Mexico City which made him grow out of patience with Diaz.

The conferences attended by Gomez were concerned with a discussion of Cabinet changes, changes in the administration of states and cities, reforms in methods of elections etc., and in the land laws. Limantour said he was unable to discuss the first point made by the revolutionists - that Diaz resign. Gomez suggested that if, as Limantour promised, there were to be changes in the personnel of the governors of some ten states, the revolutionist party be permitted to submit three names for each governorship, the federal government picking the man in each case from the names submitted by the insurgents. This, Gomez argued, was due the revolutionist party as they had demonstrated their military strength in the states under consideration. Limantour said the government would accept no such proposition and that it would name its own governors.

The conferees agreed that it was useless to talk further about details and took up the question of a preliminary conference of peace. Gomez was obdurate that the negotiations be formal and open.

The only practical effect of the conference was that Gomez wrote Francisco I. Madero, asking if he were ready to treat for peace, the conditions to be determined in the negotiations. The letter to Madero from Gomez, if it did reach the insurrecto leader, arrived within the last two or three days, though Gomez has had advices from El Paso about the difficulty of the junta there in communicating with Madero.

Senor de la Barra who was in New York at the same time as the conferences were held was invited to attend but declined, saying he did not wish to meddle in internal affairs and that his field was international. He, however, was acquainted simultaneously with the details of the situation by his colleague, Senor Limantour.

Washington Conference

Neither de la Barra nor Gomez would consent to a conference though I had frequently suggested it after the Limantour conferences in New York but when de la Barra was appointed Minister of Foreign Affairs last Sunday night, he telephoned me that he would leave the next day and I arranged to see him that night as well as the next afternoon, Sunday.

Sunday morning I went to see Gomez and discussed de la Barra's appointment with them. He had been impressed by it, I observed, and I suggested to him that inasmuch as de la Barra now was to play an important role in Mexican politics, being the premier of the Cabinet, it might not be inopportune for Gomez to explain just what the revolutionists wanted. Gomez replied that de la Barra knew well enough of their demands through Limantour who had attended the New York conferences. I suggested that de la Barra was a man of reason and justice and naught but good could come from a frank talk on the situation. Gomez consented to an informal conference.

I went to the residence of the Mexican Ambassador and laid the idea of an informal conference before de la Barra. He had informed me the night before that he would devote himself to bringing about peace in Mexico on his return there and so I took the liberty of pointing out that by a talk with Dr. Gomez, admittedly the "brains" of the revolutionist party, Senor de la Barra might become fully acquainted with the revolutionists' contentions before he tackled his new work. Senor de la Barra was busy receiving the farewells of dozens of diplomats but set everything aside and arranged to meet Gomez and myself at 3:30 p.m. We gathered in de la Barra's private library and talked for about an hour. The conversation was carried on in Spanish and as nearly as I can remember, here is what was said:

Gomez assured himself first that de la Barra was familiar with what had taken place at the New York conferences. He said he was. Gomez said the revolutionists still insisted on the resignation of Diaz as a prerequisite to peace. Senor de la Barra listened but offered no comment, saying he obviously could not discuss it for personal reasons. Gomez said the revolutionist party did not wish the immediate retirement of Diaz without some provision for a successor, adding that they realized full well anarchy might follow Diaz's abdication if not carefully planned.

Gomez outlined the demands of the revolutionists and said, in a word, that they wanted participation in governmental affairs. Cabinet changes alone would not suffice. The revolutionists wanted representation. Gomez spoke of various abuses of the courts and arbitrary acts of governors and subordinate officials of the government wherein personal and property rights often had been jeopardized. He said the only guaranty of reforms which would mean anything to the revolutionist party would be to allow them at least a minority power. Gomez instanced the workings of the bi-party system in the United States and Senor de la Barra agreed that what Mexico needed was opposite political parties. Here the Ambassador outlined the plan which was being considered in Mexico City for the establishment of a political party. (The news dispatches under date of Wednesday, March 29th from Mexico City carry this announcement but Gomez comments that it merely is a transfer from the 'cientifico' system to a new political party which is appropriating the reforms urged by the revolutionists so as to make possible the granting of the reforms by the government without recognizing the revolutionists.)

Senor de la Barra said during the conference that the government never could recognize a party of revolutionists and that political parties were founded only by peaceful methods. In discussing changes in the governorships and electoral reforms, Senor de la Barra and Gomez talked at length about methods of obtaining freedom of suffrage. Senor de la Barra said that in the forthcoming elections in the state of Puebla, the new plans might be tried out and if successful might be put into operation in Yucatan, and possibly Chihuahua where elections soon are due. This, Senor de la Barra suggested, would be evidence to the revolutionists of the sincerity of intention of the government. Gomez declared that in the two months elapsing before the elections were scheduled in Puebla, he doubted if reforms could be instituted as the people were under arms in that state and probably would remain so until all the concessions demanded by the revolutionists were granted.

Gomez wanted to know what guarantees the revolutionists would have that reforms would be carried out or that their lives would be safe from persecution if they laid down their arms. Senor de la Barra said surely political amnesty would be granted but Gomez objected to the term "amnesty", declaring that it implied a pardon when in fact the revolutionists had committed no wrong in urging reforms which the Mexican government was about to concede as just.

Senor de la Barra said that as long as he was a member of the Cabinet, he would see that justice was done. He spoke very forcibly on this point.

Both men agreed that details could better be settled in regular negotiations. Gomez reiterated that the negotiations be formal and open, and that they be held in Washington so that the revolutionists would be assured of wide publicity, the world bearing witness to the promises of the Mexican government. Senor de la Barra replied that the government never could consent to such negotiations, in Washington, because it might be construed as a recognition of belligerency and further would injure the already weakened prestige and financial credit of Mexico abroad. He added, too, that such negotiations would establish a precedent for which every dissenting party in Mexico might clamor in the future. Gomez remarked that he felt sure there never would be occasion for revolution in Mexico if the present reforms were granted.

The men parted hopeful that a modus operandi for the negotiations soon might be agreed upon. Senor de la Barra said he expected to be better able to handle the subject after his arrival in Mexico City.

****

Riding for an hour with de la Barra that night from Washington to Baltimore, he explained that the first thing he would advocate to the Cabinet would be the institution of electoral reform in Puebla. This, he said, might be followed in Yucatan and possibly Chihuahua. He was hopeful about effecting peace, saying that there would be many changes but said privately he did not believe President Diaz would resign.

David Lawrence

OCCIDENTAL CONSTRUCTION COMPANY
Office No. 704
64 Wall Street

LEWIS WARFIELD, President   New York, May 20th, 1911.

Honorable Charles D. Hilles,
        Secretary to the President,
            The White House,
                Washington, D.C.

My dear Mr. Hilles:

I have your favor of the 17th inst., and I think that I may properly tell you what I recommended to President Diaz in my telegram to him of the 11th inst., leaving out the personal part of the telegram; which was as follows:

> "My suggestion is that you modify your recent manifesto by substituting National will in place of Presidential conscience and summon all factions to form a National Committee something like the Privy Council of England with power to decide what is best for the interests of the Nation. President Roosevelt settled the great coal strike by somewhat similar procedure. Your integrity and honor are in the hearts of everybody everywhere. What they want is twentieth century government. Recent organic changes adopted by Brazil, Japan, Russia, China, England, Spain and Portugal and the new policies which Roosevelt started in our country are the reasons for my belief that my suggestions meets the real issues."

President Diaz' reply, dated 14th inst., is:-

"Mucho agradezco a su bondadosa indicacion."

Also, the telegram that I sent to Finance Minister Limantour on the same day that I wired President Diaz, was as follows:

"Answering your questions:- First - That
Washington is alive to the fact stated in my letter
April twentieth to you. The ultimate object is to
nominate Sherman for President next year. I do not
know what persons are supplying the money but
everybody can guess. Please remember that I
demonstrated to your executives six years ago that
the Harriman interests would be dangerous
concessionaires. Second - Press despatches reported
revolutionists satisfied with preliminary version but
official proclamation renewed the war. The manifesto
is regarded here as an argument. Third - Neither
army carries modern equipment for its wounded. El
Paso has supplied it for Juarez. My communications
to you are from a plain speaking friend, not from a
critic."

This in reply to his message of the same date, reading as follows:

"Message received. What do you mean trusts
exposed? Please explain more fully why manifesto
Presidente has caused bad impression. It ought to
satisfy all because it contains definite promises
resign when conditions permit. What do you mean
by victims having no medical relief?"

On the 17th inst. I sent the following telegram to Finance Minister
Limantour:

"The demand that Bonilla have portfolio of
Comunicaciones prompts me to advise you that the
interests named in telegram eleventh want primarily
annexation of Sonora and Sinaloa or secondarily
Government purchase of their constructed lines at
profitable prices."

I see by todays' newspapers that Mr. Limantour is on the verge of
collapse, therefore I do not expect further word from him on these
subjects. Todays' newspapers also state that the new Minister of
Commerce and Industry is to be Manuel Calero. He and his partner,
Vera-Estanol, are my general Counsel at the City of Mexico. The latter
accepted that portfolio when the old Cabinet resigned several weeks
ago, as well as the portfolio of Public Instruction.

It looks now to me as if President Diaz has decided that a new Cabinet to be appointed by de la Barra and Madero would accomplish the same result as the National Committee or Privy Council that I suggested. It remains to be seen if he is right. But there are other strong factions besides the Federal Government and the so-called Provisional Government represented by Madero; viz., the old faction of Reyes and the new faction represented by Figueroa. I think that President Diaz acted upon the assumption that the Reyes faction would consent to be represented by the de la Barra part of the proposed new Cabinet, and that the Figueroa faction would consent to be represented by the Madero part. It seems to me that is the real explanation for stopping General Reyes at Havana yesterday.

Personally, I think President Diaz has unconsciously opened the doors to controversy and further demands upon the present Government, some of which demands may be unlawful to comply with, by trying to bring about an adjustment in the form of pacts between the Federal Government and the Insurrecto Government. The great amount of anarchy that has already developed, together with the certain famine that will result if the crops are not put into the ground before the end of June, render it impossible to take time enough to properly consider, argue and compromise all the various questions that must be settled before committing the Government definitely to the contracts or "treaties". He would have simplified matters by telling all the factions to settle these among themselves in a joint body of a few men which would only be bound by the necessities of the situation, and not by the Constitution or the Laws. I am afraid that the method that he has adopted will forever remain as an incentive for some future revolutionary leaders to demand recognition or benefits by force of arms; whereas, the other way would always act as a blanket, because they would have to demonstrate the justice of their demands by force of argument and reason.

Nevertheless, I believe that the present peace movement has gained such an impetus now that amendments or changes in the program at Mexico City will be made to accommodate whatever differences between the factions may crop up. In other words, I believe that the general political features are virtually provided for, and that the separate States' issues will not give great trouble. Of course, contrary to the supposition of most Americans, the ideas and interests of the several States are almost as separate and distinct as we find in our country; due to the various heredities or racial characteristics, and the various classes of industries or agriculture.

The danger that looms on the horizon, to my mind, can best be expressed by the old saying: "The scramble for the pork when hog-killing time comes". I am afraid that is why Mr. Limantour will not retain his portfolio when the proposed joint Cabinet is formed (supposing yesterday's newspaper despatches are correct). They could stop the raid on the Treasury by instituting a Court of Claims, of course, but the crops have got to be planted before the end of June or else there will be a famine next Autumn; and undoubtedly the rank and file of the insurrectos will not give up a sure support from the Government until their claims for compensation are paid or definitely agreed to.

Hoping that what I have said may throw some light on the subject for the benefit of the President, I remain,

Sincerely yours,

Lewis Warfield

REBEL ATTACK IN ZACATECAS

On the morning of May 20th last, at 5 o'clock, about five hundred Carransistas made an attack on the Federal garrison, consisting of some hundred odd men, stationed in Concepcion del Oro, Zacatecas, where the copper smelter of the Mazapil Copper Company is located. The attack started at five o'clock, as stated, and ended at 8:30 a.m., resulting in the taking of the town and a complete Carransista victory. The dead amounted to about forty and the wounded about fifteen, consisting of both Federals and Rebels, as well as non-combatants. Sixty Federal prisoners were taken, the capitan of whom was executed eight days later. The Federal garrison consisted of about forty infantry and sixty odd rurales or cavalrymen. The infantry surrendered at about seven o'clock after their lieutenant had been killed. At this time the firing on both sides, fighting around the main plaza ceased, when two of the rebels fell, directly across the street in front of the main office building of the Company, one of them being slightly wounded in one arm, while the other received a mortal wound. Immediately the cry went up from the rebels that they were being fired upon from the building of the Company, and they again began firing, not on the Federals, but at the office building of the Company. I should judge that at least two hundred rifle shots struck the walls of this building, as well as entering the windows both of the upper and lower stories. The upper story is used as private quarters for the Assistant Manager of the Company, where, if he had been at the time, with his family, they surely would have all been killed, as the sleeping rooms were riddled, bullets penetrating most of the furniture contained in them. Fortunately, the Assistant Manager was on the back porch, protected by two adobe walls, with his family, when this occurred. The rebels then made a rush for the main gate of the smelter grounds, wherein were collected most of the foreign employees of the Company, and about fifty of them entered, shouting "Death to the Gringos". Just inside of the smelter, and to the left of the main gate, behind the double walls of the main office building, they encountered the small group of foreigners, with their several families, where they had congregated for protection from the flying bullets. Some of them then entered the building of the Company from the rear [several words illegible] foreign shooters, whom they claimed had fired upon them. Two of them, at least, opened fire on the small group of defenseless foreigners, men, women and children. From eight to twelve shots were fired at them by the rebels, from a distance of fifteen to twenty feet, and the only manner in which I can account for the fortunate escape from bullets of those uninjured, is that the rebels did not raise their rifles to the shoulder to take aim, but fired rather hurriedly from the hip. The first shot missed, by a very narrow margin, the head of one of the men, who turned and ran for the corner of the adjacent building. He was the aim of two more bullets, as he ran, one of which struck the corner, just as he ran around it. Then another rebel, just behind the first shooter, opened fire, the bullet from whose rifle passed through the hands of a man in front of me, and struck the wall, close to where I was standing, an inch or two to one side of my right leg. I jumped through the first convenient door which happened to be that of the kitchen of Mr. Clapham, shoving my wife on ahead of me, and carrying my baby in my arms. I heard several more rifle reports, as we ran on into the adjoining rooms, the last one seeming to have been discharged within the house, and was accompanied by a groan. Suffice to state that my wife and I, with the baby escaped to another part of the smelter grounds.

On my return to the scene of the shooting, about ten minutes after, I found that Mr. Clapham, Master Mechanic for the Company, had been the recipient of a rifle bullet, in the upper fleshy-part of his right leg, on the inside, the ball entering from the back and leaving a bad wound where it came out, from the effects of which, I understand, that Mr. Clapham will probably loose his foot.

I desire to state that none of the foreign employees fired on the Rebels, or made any resistance, in any manner what-so-ever. Most of those who entered the smelter appeared to be intoxicated and completely beyond control, nor did I see any officer with them at the time, although I was informed afterwards, that a rebel leader did enter and gave them a command to cease firing.

Further than this incident, the foreigners were not molested, but were well treated and given proper consideration by the Leader in Charge, Don Eulalio Gutierrez.

****

The above was written by R. E. Young, American Citizen, Chief Clerk of the Mazapil Copper Company.

John R. Silliman,
Vice Consul

C O N F I D E N T I A L

December 14, 1911.

CONFIDENTIAL MEMORANDUM FOR GENERAL WOOD:
(IN RE MEXICO)

Sentimentalism, pure and simple, put the present man in the presidency. He is a curious mixture--more headstrong than strong of character, an amateur in politics rather than a tried statesman. He appears seeking to establish a government on a misunderstood Machiavellian principle. In his Prince Machiavelli demonstrated how, by dividing forces against themselves, one could rule. This man seems to be seeking to unite factional opposition against himself by dividing all the different elements from himself. To win the masses to his revolutionary cause he made promises that any tyre in statesmanship and state economics must have known could not be kept; promises about dividing the land among the people. This coming on top of Limantour's suggestion that certain great estates be divided among the people gave special point to these promises. Limantour threw out the suggestion to embarrass Henry Clay Creel, whose lands it was proposed so generously to divide, and to lead the revolutionists into that political bog. In this way the people are cajoled at the expense of the upper classes. Bandits like Zapata are permitted a free hand, and tried soldiers and officers insulted--discriminated against and discouraged until many trained officers out of self-respect resign from the army.

Thus the democratic spirit is outraged by the forcing upon the states state officials the people do not want, and upon the country a vice president who is so unpopular that when the presidential inauguration took place he was not allowed to be present lest his wide unpopularity would cause a demonstration of disapproval that might overflow on the Presidential candidate himself and make impossible a carefully organized demonstration of popular approval of himself. Finally, when the laboring element petitioned him to seek the passage of a law establishing an eight-hour a day working day, instead of putting that delicate problem up to an adverse congress and letting them settle the question and their own fate, he forgets all statesmanship in opposing the measure and in contemplating his own economic theory and with this fine decisive unwisdom sets the laboring element of Mexico against him.

Fearful of the confidence and popularity won by the provisional President through his wise administration of the provisional government, he proceeds through his newspaper organs and political jobbers to undermine and blacken the reputation of the one man who seems to possess the confidence and respect of all the best elements of the people, openly charging him with double dealing and conspiring with Reyes against himself, supporting the charge with evidence so flimsy and patently manufactured that even the impulsive Latin-American is not deceived by it. All the strongest and reputable men of the country are into silence or exile by his blatant charges of conspiracy. Hundreds of his countrymen are proscribed and largely because of their political opinions, and this sort of oppression is not confined to men, but even extended to women. The constitutional independence of the States as well as the individual is threatened. As the result, factions are being united against him and already in Congress there is a threat of impeachment of the new president. Small wonder that there exists widespread doubt of the possibility of the establishment of a firm government under the existing conditions. But when one remembers to what condition the country was brought by thirty years of tyranny--a tyranny so progressively oppressive as to have finally broken into the conflagration of spontaneous revolt, which has arisen rather through force of circumstances rather than any marked ability of his own, and which caught up Madero on its storm and made him chief rider--one can hardly believe that any attempt to establish a constitutional government would meet with success. I am convinced that a far stronger man would have faced failure, and that even the Provisional President, had his power been final rather than provisional, would have been wrecked by the raging storm of political chaos so inevitable after so long a period of political subjugation. As it was, de la Barra's power was but provisional, and all the political parties welcomed the inauguration of Madero for the division of the spoils and the distribution of the plans. It was evident that where one could be satisfied thousands must be disappointed. Only a great man, or a combination of irresistable circumstances could possibly hope for success under such conditions. The course of current events is as natural as it is inevitable.

Reyes, whose name is being used to head the new revolution, is simply like a masque at a carnival, worn to cover the real faces. As intimately as I know General Reyes, I am bound to say that he is beginning to be universally distrusted because of his propensity to leave his followers in the lurch at the critical moment.

CONFIDENTIAL

Political Situation in Mexico

A friction has come between Congress and the Executive. Deputy Uruehurtu, a Corral man, introduced a bill to the Chamber of Deputies, summoning before the chamber the Ministers of Justice, of War and of the Interior, to give an account of wholesale assassination of Reyistas leaders by the troops and of the mistreatment of three journalists in Hermosillo, capital of the State of Sonora, where, according to Uruehurtu, one of the journalists was tied to a wagon with a rope and dragged through the streets and the two others were banished by the authorities. Banishment is forbidden by the constitution. The Chamber approved the bill and the Secretaries were summoned.

The following day the Secretaries sent a communication to the Chamber professing to ignore the said assassinations and the mistreatment of journalists--stating that the executive opinion was that the chamber had no authorization to summon the secretaries. This statement stirred the chamber and after a warm discussion the Chamber's summons to the Secretaries were approved and they were again summoned; also a motion to reform the regulations of the Chamber to make clear the faculties of the Chamber to summon the ministers whenever it was advisable to do so was approved.

"Nueva Era", the organ of President Madero as the result of this action, published a bitter article against the Congress stating that all of its members are more tools of the regime of Diaz and suggesting the dissolution of the Congress. There is no doubt that the President has a bitter opposition in the Congress and that a friction exists between the executive and legislative powers.

Pasqual Orozco, the revolutionary leader, now a General in Chihuahua commanding troops, publishes a telegram in the newspapers of Mexico City dated the 7th, protesting against the statement that he is in connivance with Reyes. The telegram is as follows:

"The Daily El Norto publishes a telegram of the Associated Press stating that some officials of the United States say they have knowledge that I am engaged in the Reyista movement and that my secretary has been in constant communication with the Reyista junta at El Paso. Everybody who knew myself and my secretary will know that we are incapable of doing the infamies they attribute to us and therefore they will know that the statements made in the telegram mentioned are a falsehood and I denied it publicly according to my honesty. As I said some time ago, my mission as a military commander is to be loyal to the constitutional government."

****

Benito Juarez, Governor of Oaxaca, won great prestige all over the country on account of his firm attitude defending the sovereignty of the State. The leader of the Indians of Juchitan, Jose Gomez, was imprisoned and shot in spite of a passport that President Madero gave him enabling him to go safely to Mexico. That was done by the troops of the State of Oaxaca, commanded by Governor Juarez.

General Ambrosio Figueroa, one of the principal leaders of the revolution, published a letter criticising the attitude of Governor Juarez and offering Madero his services against the people of Oaxaca. Figueroa is the provisional governor of the State of Morelos now disturbed by Zapata and his bands of bandits. Pascual Orozco sent a telegram congratulating Figueroa for his letter and offering also to President Madero his services against governor of Oaxaca, Benito Juarez.

The letter of Figueroa and the telegram of Orozco, was a grave mistake on the part of both. The people of Oaxaca have always been very proud and independent. The letter of Figueroa stirred all the inhabitants of Oaxaca. The leading women of the State published a letter in the Imparcial challenging Figueroa and Orozco, to go to Oaxaca and fight with them. "Without aid of our men", state the women, "we will be able to prove to you the heroism of our people." This incident has brought about a friction between the inhabitants of Oaxaca and those of Morelos, the State where Figueroa was born. On the other hand, Figueroa and Orozco have been criticized with reason.

****

Disturbances are growing principally on the border with the United States and in the south. Elections are pending in Puebla where the local Congress will designate the governor because none of the candidates obtained a majority and in the State of Veza Cruz. In all probability in these two States the disturbances will increase.

****

Messrs. Smith and John DeKay visited the office of the Commercial Agent complaining that the government revoked a decree of the Secretary of the Interior of last June, thereby endangering the interest of the National Mexican Packing Company, Limited, which amounts to ten million dollars. They say this action of the government will bring a financial scandal.

LETTER TO MR. H. L. SWAIN

IN REGARD TO

CONDITIONS IN MEXICO.

Extract from Letter to Mr. H. L. Swain from
Superintendent of the Refugio Gold and Silver Mine,
Zacatetas.
****

"I believe it is very dangerous for you to come and also very difficult. The work here has stopped and there is no change since my last letter to you. The Government is doing nothing in the matter of helping small towns here at all. A few days ago we were surrounded by a troop and so close to us that the greater part of the superintendents and employees of the hill ranches have abandoned everything because it is much more dangerous to stay than to go away, and the Government is not sending any soldiers to aid the haciendas or ranches. And for that reason the rebels are pursuing their course as they please, committing all kinds of depredations and such things. In Pinos the troops have risen in arms against the Government and are robbing all that they can. They have robbed all the officers in the town, let out the prisoners and they have joined together with them making about 100 men in all. They are now doing much damage over this part of the country. They have just finished the ranches of San Martin and La Trinidad, and yesterday between two and three o'clock they were fighting in the ranch of La Pendencia. At this moment I do not know the result of fighting in Pendencia, nor the number of men there or how many there are at this moment in all parts of the country, but it is impossible to do anything because the workmen are very unquiet. The Government has not lent any aid nor sent a soldier, while daily the town people are sending messages to the Government in Mexico City, they do not even answer them. As you can understand, it will be an impossibility that you could come up and much less that you could start up the work again within a short time. All around us here with the better people they are frightened to death, but this will not last long because as soon as they have robbed all the haciendas and stolen all there is to be stolen they will have to leave for other parts. Then we will be in possession again and I will advise you at once so you can come up and start work.

This property that this letter was from is in the southern part of the State of Zacatetas, very close to the line of San Luis Potosi. It is reached by several lines, from Aguascalientes or from San Luis Potosi, and the railroad station is Salinas. Outside of a very few visits from the rebels in the last two years, it has been very quiet. The first time, during the Madero revolution, two years ago I think in April, there was a bandit came in and took the City of Salinas, robbed everything, took some of the foreigners and maltreated them. In Salinas there was a large salt works, run by an English company. The man that was in charge there was the son of a lord, name is Stanhope, I think. He was very elderly man, over sixty I guess. The time that they were there, the bandits took him out of the house and to the railroad tracks and made him run up and down that railroad track for two hours and then they took him and put him in a box car that was there, shut him in and kept him there all day without anything to eat. After they had stolen all he had, and killed several horses, they demanded 5,000 pesos. I think they got about a thousand. There were some American boys there and they took them out in back of the power plant and demanded fifty dollars apiece from them. The boys said they did not have any money, said they might get it, and they all talked it over about an hour, I guess, and at last one of the boys said, "Let me go to town and I will try to get it". They gave him a half hour to go to town, and if he did not come back they would shoot this man and also hunt him up. The boy went down and got the money and they let him go. This bandit was afterwards caught, I think, about two weeks after that, and they found over 50,000 pesos on him that he had stolen. He was nothing but a peon when he started in.

After that, we had no trouble up in that neighborhood until the February trouble in Mexico City. This man Aguenedo came in with 800 men and stopped there a week. He did not do any damage himself but there was quite a good deal of damage done. They took all the live stock and horses before he left. We thought that was the end of all trouble, as we never had had any trouble before except with the bandits. Until about a week ago, or two weeks ago, when those troops at Pinos revolted and started out, everything was quiet. They will be there, I think, only a short time, as there will be nothing else for them to eat and then they will leave. San Luis Potosi is in a pretty bad way. The Maderista governor of San Luis Potosi was taken prisoner after the Huerta government took charge. He had a carload of rifles that he had been carrying during the Madero regime and was just about ready to rise in arms when he was arrested and taken down to Mexico and put in prison for a while. He was released and went up to try and get Carranza to stop, but stayed up there a short time, then came back and went off.

The border states are bad, even Chihuahua. The government does not hold control of any of the northern states today; possibly they hold that State of Chihuahua, but that is about all I guess. They hold Juarez, but Juarez is just a small place right at the border and opposite El Paso. They have no customs houses in the country except at Vera Cruz and Tampico on this coast. Along the border between the Gulf and the Gulf of California they have nothing. Practically all, except Juarez, is in the hands of the rebels, and Juarez is just as good as lost because railway communication is shut off entirely.

The people are all for politics, every one of them. There is not an honest one among them. Felix Diaz is the most honest one. He has stood by everything he has promised. I really think that so far as the country is concerned that Huerta is trying to clear things up. I think he wants to see the country in peace, but he wants to be dictator. Once they get this load they will start right in and do something. Congress has passed the law, and according to what I find out, they are making arrangements through England to get their money. They are very peculiar people and they have to be treated just like children, from the highest down to the lowest. I can take the peons and, I believe, do anything with them by treating them right. The next man will try to drive them and he will not do at all. Treat them like children and you can get them to do anything you want. I have been twenty years among them and never had any trouble with a one of them. You will find that all these foreigners, especially the Germans, have been killed on account of the treatment they have given to the natives. The Germans here are very hard on these people, treating them worse than slaves. There was a manager of a sugar plantation killed here last fall, and it was his own fault. The way he treated the natives, cheating them out of their pay, and fining them, caused them as soon as they got a chance they gave it to him. Every case of a foreigner that has been killed or been molested in any way you can trace it back to mistreatment of the people. In hundreds of cases, if the natives are treated halfway decent there will never by any trouble. I would not be afraid to go into the Zapatistas' country, nor afraid of the rebels, as they would not molest me. It is simply the way you treat them. They will molest their own people quicker than they will a foreigner. There have been a few cases up North where they have held people for ransom, but down here they do not.

Take the case of Mr. Platt, which it seems to me came out in the English papers some time ago. Mr. Platt has charge of mining property in Zacualpan, State of Mexico, about ten or twelve hours ride from Toluca. Several months ago the rebels came in toward him, and he and all his men, two foreigners beside himself, with beds and bedding and food, etc., went right into the mine and all waited there until the rebels came up. When the rebels came, he went out to meet them to have a talk with them. They immediately took him in charge and demanded a ransom of 5,000 pesos, and he being unable to pay it they took him along. They then started for the town of Zacualpan, which is about an hour's ride from the mine, with the intention of taking this town from the Government forces. They kept Mr. Platt in the lead of the procession and when he did not go willingly they jogged his memory with a bayonet in the back. After reaching the outskirts of the town they sent word in demanding its surrender, giving them until evening, I think. The people in Zacualpan were ready for them, however, and instead of receiving them with open hands, commenced firing at them. As soon as the firing commenced, they placed Mr. Platt in the front ranks. When the firing started all around he said he was at first a little afraid, but after the shooting kept up for a few minutes he felt better in the front than at the rear, and he stayed there. The firing kept up for a short while, when the forces from Zacualpan made a sortie, throwing dynamite bombs into the ranks of the rebels. This scared them so that they ran, and as soon as they ran one way Mr. Platt ran the other. It took him about four hours to get to a place called Losacas, the headquarters of the company for which he was working. At Losacas they were rather frightened because they had heard the shooting.

These bombs or grenades that were used are, I think, about one and one-half inches in diameter and about 6 inches long. The inside is filled with guncotton, and at the top end there is a percussion cap screwed in, and at the lower end there is a piece of wire the size of the gun and sufficiently long enough to touch the cartridge. They use a cartridge where the ball has been taken out and soap put in - a regular Mauser cartridge. It is fired like any rifle, but the bomb does not go very far, perhaps 200 yards is the limit. Around the edge of the bomb on the outside is a ring of iron, cut into clips, and as soon as the bomb bursts the iron ring bursts itself and goes all around. These bombs, I think, are made in England. The last night of the fight on the 18th of February in Mexico City, I was near the Embassy, and at about three o'clock in the morning there were three of these bombs that went off in Chapultepeo Avenue, about a block away from the Embassy, and from the sound I thought they were dynamite. First you hear the rifle going off and about a half a minute later, probably less, you hear the dynamite bomb go off, making a noise like a cannon. At close firing these do a lot of damage. The wire used looks like regular brass telephone wire, and is about the size of the barrel of a Mauser. They insert it in the barrel of the rifle, so that it touches the cartridge, no air coming in, and the exploding of the cartridge sends it off like a bullet. We tried to find out who were firing these things, but could not find out anything. There were about three of them in about 20 minutes. I think it was the Government soldiers. I have one of these bombs that did not go off.

The troops of Zapata are like devils. They are mostly Indians, and they have degenerated so much in the last twenty or forty years that they are simply animals. All they think of is getting money enough to dress up nice and have plenty to eat and plenty of girls around. They take charge of the girls and young married women, where there are any in a town, and use them until they are through and then throw them aside. That is not only in one section, but all over the Republic, north, east, south and west. The Maderistas also did it the time they took Culiacan, the capital of the state of Sinaloa. When they took that town, they just cleaned it right out, women, girls and everything they could put their hands on. The same thing happened in the Zapatistas' country in the State of Mexico. The time they took Cuatlan they started to drink hard, and when they got drunk they went around to the houses and gathered up the young women and girls and took them to the biggest house they could find, with the biggest rooms. They made them undress, and when some of them refused they tore their clothes right off of them. The people in Cuatlan stayed in their houses and did not raise a hand. Never in any place that I know of, have they done otherwise. That shows what kind of people they are. They haven't much feeling for women anyhow, and treat them like slaves. Even the higher classes, that call themselves gentlemen, and are married, all have a mistress somewhere. They cannot be true to their wives and families, and the wives know it. I suppose their wives do the same thing.

In Salio, when Huerta went against the Carranzistas, they went around the houses and gathered up all the young women and girls and young married people, took them to the City Hall and locked them up, and then went around to their parents and husbands and told them that unless they would pay them so much money they would turn their soldiers in on these women and children. Fortunately they had a little money. They paid them that, but outside of giving them the money, they did not try to stop them. I think the classes in the North are the stronger and better class of people than here, possibly on account of the difference in climate. But they are more civilized in the wrong way.

Take any Mexican, and ninety-nine cases out of a hundred he is a coward. Of course, there are a few exceptions. But let them get drunk, and when they do so, they are not afraid of anything - they get crazy. That has been my experience. They are bad enough sober, but it is nothing compared to them when they get drunk. They all carry knives or machetes. About 99% of them get drunk whenever there is an opportunity. I never met a Mexican that wouldn't get drunk. And the women have to stand it. I have seen women carrying their men - a few are married in this country - and when they get them out of town for a mile or two, they lay them down by the side of the road and let them sleep it off. The women will stay there for anywhere from three to eight hours at a time. Then the man will wake up and see the woman there and hit her, sending her flying about ten feet, but she will come right back every time. I have seen that. That is the way they treat their wives or women. Of course, I don't mean the men of higher education and station, but men of the peon class. There is a middle class, composed of peons that have received a little education in the past ten years. This class only came up in the last ten years - before that there were only two classes. But the middle class are only a little better than the lowest. If this trouble keeps up though, they will go back, as they cannot get any more work. They work on the railroads and in the manufacturing businesses. They can read and understand mechanics, etc.

The war has got to come, and I hope it will be known in time so that everything can be made ready. The Mexican Railway Co. here will always be ready to give any help they have got. They have enough engines here and at Orizaba and Cordova - of course. Cordova is only a few miles from here. They always have enough freight cars here and a few passenger cars - enough to get quite a crowd up there. You do not have to take horses, as you won't need them, and besides there are not any horses hardly, mostly mules. The telegraph lines could be out so that no word would reach Mexico City of your coming. The worst part of the trip would be to the top of the mountain - when you get up there, then three-fourths of the work is done. It is practically down hill from there to Mexico City. There are hundreds of automobiles in Mexico City owned by foreigners. There are two or three railroad lines from Esparansa into Mexico City, one of them narrow gauge. There is not a line between Mexico and Puebla, and Puebla is cut off entirely. You could make the trip from here to Mexico City in 12 or 24 hours – double the time it takes to run there today. Puebla is the worst City in the whole republic – they are always fighting. As for the number of troops in Mexico City, it is hard to say. They are always coming and going. Probably between 5000 and 6000 troops there.

In case of intervention they say that they will all unite against the foreigners and fight for their country. I do not think, however, that they would fight any more against foreigners than against their brothers. Of course, there would be a few. And in the second place, lots of these people have not carried arms in the past few years. Thousands of them have never had a gun in hand. Take any of these and try to put them in the army or a regular corps and what is the result? We all know what practice means, as nearly every one shoots high when shooting at a man.

I am of the opinion that anybody that went into the country would have no trouble. There has been talk of 250,000 men taking ten years to conquer. I think from 50,000 to 75,000 troops, well armed, could clear this country in two or three years. The Filipinos are 100% worse than the people here. The people here are not as treacherous. I have been through the country here during the trouble, and a great part of the time I start out very early in the morning about 2 or 3 o'clock. I have gone through these villages where they have an armed force belonging to the Government, and at all times I have had not less than three or four men with me as guard. And at no time while passing through these villages at night have I ever been molested, called at, or has any officer or soldier shown his head outside of the door or window to see who was coming. And these are the little towns where the Zapatistas are expected to come in at any moment. It is a fact, never have I been with anybody but what they have spoken about the same thing. They never keep a guard up. When marching from one place to another, they never keep a picket line for any flank movements, etc. They are ambushed time after time, but never take any heed of it. These are both Federals and Zapatistas that do this.

Undoubtedly, I think that Pasqual Orozco, when he gets North will join the rebels under Carranza. I do not understand why they ever sent him. He took a good many men and rifles. Maybe they will not join the rebels at once, but he has done it once and I do not see why he will not do it again. He was a strong Maderista at first. He was the one that took Juarez, which practically settled the question of the first revolution, and after Madero got in, I suppose it was three months after that that Orozco went against him. That is what caused that fight, and if it had not been for those big guns that the Government had, there is no question but that Orozco would have won out.

As for the number of guns I cannot say. Some of them are 80 millimetres, or three inch. They are field guns. Some are double barrel guns, French guns, I believe. I think they have some mortars too. I know an 80 millimetre gun was the largest they had in Mexico City, and suppose that is the largest they have. They must have, I suppose, 200 or 300 of them. I think they are sending a good many into Morelos and Sonora and some up North, and probably they have not over 100 in Mexico City. There are a great many machine guns there, I don't know how many. Hotchkiss or French machine guns.

The Americans in Mexico are not organized, but we have an organization in Mexico City.

As to what is going to be done in Mexico now, I cannot tell you. I do think that as soon as the present government get their money, the loan that I spoke of, they will go right ahead and try to clear up the country. I think Huerta wants to make a show of it, now that he is at the head, and I think he wants to clear up the country as quick as he can. But he cannot do that unless he gets money, but just as soon as he gets it I think there will be something doing. The troops do not enthuse unless they get money. As I said, I think 50,000 to 75,000 American troops can clean the whole country up, and it would not take them over 2 or 3 years to do it. I think the idea of 250,000 troops in 10 years is foolish. We could not expect any help, and I think that the Mexicans would simply remain dormant. Zapata we could wipe out in 2 months. The great trouble has been that the government troops could not get up with him. This is the way they fight. Huerta could have whipped Orozco in about 2 months or 2 weeks, if he had wanted to. When Huerta went up and after the first fight, Orozco retreated about 10 or 20 miles. Huerta went up to the position that Orozco had occupied - it was fortified - and stayed there a month. After he got ready again and the troops were all rested, he started after Orozco again. He kept that up for about 4 months, whereas if he had done as any fighting country would have done, just as soon as he had started that fellow going he would have kept him going. They would do the same thing with Zapata and are doing the same thing with Carranza. These are facts, not hearsay. Whenever they march in a town after capturing it, they stay there a month or so to celebrate the victory. The officers give banquets and the soldeirs steal what drinks they can and three-fourths of them get drunk. Of course, of the irregular troops they have no command of them at all. The irregular troops and officers are practically nothing more than peons.

I saw Orozco about 15 years ago - had nothing to do with him but just saw him. This was about 6 or 8 years before he went to fight for Madero. He had a pack train and used to take the silver bullion from the mines in Chihuahua down to the railroad station. He did that and his father did it. His father has done it for about 40 years. He was a man that could hardly read or write, and now I believe Orozco is one of the best educated men in the whole lot of these rebels. Aguenedo is a man that never could read or write. My superintendent used to know the fellow when he was in the cotton fields. He was in Salinas at the time Aguemedo went there and acted as his secretary. Sent all of Aguemedo's papers and all his messages and knows what occurred there. He knows that Aguemedo could not even sign his name. I suppose Orozco is the best educated rebel. That is the class of men you would have to deal with.

I think two or three trainloads of men could get from here to Mexico City in a short time. It would take about 1500 or 2000 fighting men to clean the city out, and they could do it in no time at all. It is said that the Ciudadela is impregnable. I do not believe it. There are blocks of houses leading to the Ciudadela in all directions, all being adobe houses. As far as the Ciudadela is concerned, in 2 or 3 days, according to how many men you have, you could take that easily.

You would have to take the Plaza. Scott did that when he went into the town. Went right over wall after wall until he got his men into the Plaza and then you command nearly all streets. You could drill right through the walls. They are nothing but mud and I think a four foot wall could be entered in about 15 minutes.

I suppose the government has about 10,000 soldiers right now. Until lately, they were not organized at all. Now they are organizing very much under the rules of the United States Army. Before, their organization was in zones, North Zone, South Zone, East Zone and West Zone. A brigadier general or some other high official was in command of a zone, and he had a certain number of men, depending upon the part of the country they were in, either artillery, cavalry or infantry. Most of the big guns they kept in Mexico City. Now, under the reorganization of Huerta, the army is divided into divisions, each division complete, either cavalry, artillery or infantry, with field guns and rapid fire guns for each division. They have five or six of these divisions now. I suppose the regular army is supposed to be about 60,000. Now, each State capital has its regiment of soldiers, federal troops, and all of these regiments have their band and the band plays in the Plaza three or four times a week.

If all of these younger fellows in Mexico City, who claim that they belong to the higher class, could go into the Army as officers, I imagine they all would do so, but they will not go in and fight with the peons. The Mexican Army today is composed of nothing more than prisoners. Some few peons have been brought in, but I suppose nine-tenths of them are prisoners. They take these Zapatistas that they capture in Morelos, put them in jail, and drill them about a month, and then send them out to Sonora to fight the rebels in Sonora. That is the way they have done straight along. And, of course, the soldiers do not care whether they fight or not. Nine out of ten, when they get to Sonora and get a chance, will go over to the other side. Now, I believe, they have passed a law for compulsory military service, and they have started in to make regulations that they should have made two years ago. They hope before the end of the year to have things in a position that they can start compulsory service.

If the United States should intervene, I think that all the foreigners are liable to be killed - that is as quick as it is known. It would take some time for the news to spread. Not only Americans, but all foreigners would be in danger. They do not know the difference between English and Americans or Germans and Americans. This new scheme that has come up might affect us in some way - that is, when Huerta called on the Ambassador and said he would not recognize him any longer unless the United States would recognize the government.

We have been hurt too by the proclamations that President Taft made. He made some proclamation last year to American citizens, advising them what to do and stating that under no conditions would there ever be intervention. It is impossible to know how much that has hurt us. The people have an entirely different feeling toward us. Before, they used to respect us. You would not notice it, but I notice it; there is a difference in treatment. Taft also sent one or two messages to the Mexican Government telling them what they must do and what they must not do, and that if they did not do it that the United States would have to take action. The Mexican Government answered

one of them in a pretty stiff way and the other they did not take any
notice of. That was some time last fall, I don't remember when. It was
caused, I think, on account of the trouble around Cannanea, the first
trouble. When we sent in arms for the protection of foreigners in
Cannanea, about that time. It seems to me that the message stated in
effect that unless the Mexican Government could protect American
citizens, that something would be done.

The Northern States want to secede. Those along the border want
annexation to the United States. They are more capable of
self-government there than they are here. More Americanized. They are
a better class of people. It was practically all cut and dried for these
Northern states to secede whether Madero lost out or not. They were
nearly ready to secede, and the plans nearly all made when this trouble
came off in Mexico City. The only trouble is that Huerta did not get all
of them quick enough. He got the Governor of Chihuahua, but he did
not get Carranza or the governor of Sonora. These rebels are the only
armed troops that were under Madero. Madero had been sending
ammunition and men by the carload to them, they stating that the
country was in very bad shape, and they are the ones under Carranza
now.

Zapata has got practically all of Morelos, the southern part of
Mexico, and the eastern and south-eastern parts of the state of Puebla.

Diaz is the best man for president, after Huerta, but he is not
strong enough, too honest and too much law and order. There cannot
be law and order in this country at the present time. That is where
Madero fell down.

The present cabinet is, I suppose, as strong as they can get.
There are factions - too many factions, though. Diaz has a faction,

Orozco has a faction. Grenados is the most honest man in the whole
cabinet. The Minister of Gubernacion is too quick tempered, and is a
man who has to be allowed to have his own way in everything. He is in
trouble all the time. The Minister of Communicacion, Guentas, is for
Orozco. Reyes and Montregon are for Diaz. I think de la Barra is in
what is known as the Catholic faction. I think de la Barra is a good
man for the place he is in. Montregon I don't think much of. I think if
there is any trouble today that Montregon would not be with Felix Diaz.
The barracks are all for the different leaders, some for Diaz, some for
Huerta, some for Reyes and some for Montregon. They are divided so
that it is hard to tell who is who. I don't think Huerta knows how many
men he could count on. Nobody knows what Blanquet will do. He was
on the fence during the whole ten days fight - nobody knows what he
was going to do. He kept his mouth shut, and did not say a word until
the last moment. He is in charge of the Mexico City forces, and a good
general. I do not think Blanquet would go against Diaz because Porfirio
Diaz made him what he is today. I think there is only one form of
government to be had - that of a dictatorship. It would require a much
larger army today than it would thirty days ago, because the country
is more divided. Telegraphic communication is so bad that it would be
hard to know who is on one side and who is on the other. The
dictatorship should be more liberal than that of Porfirio Diaz and should
educate the people. They are not capable of any other form of
government. I think that is what Huerta is trying to do. The greatest
wrong the United States is doing is in not recognizing the republic.
Mexico is really a border state and if the United States upholds the
Monroe Doctrine, she has got to look on Mexico as one of her children,
practically. She is not doing it the way things are going now. That is
the way we look at it now. There is no reason why the government
should not be recognized - it is just as legal as if a president had been
elected. There was a man coming through here the first of the week. I
asked him what they think of the situation up in New York and why
they do not recognize Mexico and he said "I guess it is because they
killed Madero". But that was a necessity. Our people cannot understand
it, I could not understand it, but living here as I do I know that it

was necessary, because if he had not been killed he would have been in arms today. We have got to look at their doings in their own way to a certain extent. This is a military regime and a military regime is the only one that is going to be successful.

Everybody knows that Zapata was directly kept up by the Mexican Government in the Madero Regime. That was done for financial reasons of course. The Madero family desired to buy a large sugar plantation in Morelos, and Zapata was kept going with the idea of bothering those people all he could, looting, robbing small towns and banks, and after the officers got their share of the money, the soldiers got the rest.

Several months ago, one morning about four o'clock, a taxicab was found on the side of the road near Mexico City. The driver of the taxi had been shot and the mechanic killed also. It was a mystery for a great while, and it eventually came up that the killing was done by Gustavo Madero and his companion. The reason was that the Government of Mexico had taken out in this auto four boxes of rifle ammunition to aid Zapata, and coming back, these two men were shot simply because they knew of the transaction. This is on the records.

During the ten days fight, Gustavo Madero and Francisco Madero had made a list of about thirty people in Mexico City who were to be taken out and shot. Among them were Grenadas, Estambione and Lozano, also de la Barra. De la Barra had to go into the English legation where he stayed for the last four days of the fight, because he was afraid. They even tried to get him in the legation. They went out to call on him and asked for a meeting, but he refused. The men sent to call on him were searched and they were armed. Grenadas went out beyond Mexico City to a suburb and hid himself there. One night a message came out to the house where he was hiding, informing him that two congressmen would be out to search the place and take him the next day. He left and went to some other hiding place. The next morning, two deputies went out and had the place searched and not finding Grenadas arrested the man that had him hid. This man disclaimed all knowledge, but he was kept in prison until after the trouble was over. He would have been shot. They also tried to kill Huerta twice, by poison and by shooting.

In case Huerta is successful in establishing his government, I do not know what action Diaz will take. The agreement is now that the elections will be held in October next, and at that time Huerta hopes to have the country at peace so he will be able to turn it over to Diaz in good shape. I doubt whether Diaz will ever be President. I think that Huerta will be elected by the people in the elections. But the elections are always false, Madero's was too.

As to there being any magazines or supply depots in Mexico City in case of war, I would say there are none. The troops never have a commissary but depend on the women of the soldiers. Suppose on a march to Mexico City. The soldiers would go ahead of the troops, rob everything there is to rob, then squat down, make fires, prepare the food and wait for the troops to come up.

*   *   *   *   *   *   *

Guanajuato, Mexico.
January 4, 1913.

To Senator Wesley L. Jones,
Washington, D.C., U.S.A.

My dear Senator:

I am enclosing you herewith a letter based on my observations in Mexico during a period of over twenty years.

I think I told you that my sister came to Mexico about twenty-five years ago as a missionary for the Women's Foreign Missionary Society and has resided here ever since. After being here in that capacity for several years, she married, and her husband has been in active business, and was U.S. Consular Agent for Guanajuato for fifteen years.

We have all been interested in the real development and uplifting of the Mexican, and try to look at conditions unbiased by commercial reasons.

Please consider this letter confidential, as I do not want it to be published, as some references might provoke criticism here with officials. If you wish to show the letter to Senator Bristow or any others who will treat it confidentially, there will be no objection to so doing.

I expect my family here in a week to stay all winter. We have confidence that the difference between Mexico and the U.S. will be honorably adjusted.

Yours truly,

M. K. Rodgers.

Guanajuato, Mexico.
January 4, 1913.

To Senator Wesley L. Jones,
Washington, D.C., U.S.A.

My dear Senator:

Referring to our conversation in Washington last May about Mexico, I thought you might be interested in some additional information about present conditions.

I came to Mexico first twenty years ago and have had business interests here ever since, and during this time have travelled over 30,000 miles in Mexico and have gained some knowledge of Mexican conditions and especially the progress being made by Mexico.

Last winter I called on President Madero soon after his election, being taken to the palace by Don Francisco Madero, the President's father. The President and his father sat side by side and talked in English very hopefully about their new responsibilities. During the conversation, the President said, holding up his right arm: "My predecessor ruled by the strong arm, but I propose to rule with justice," and spoke very positively that within three months the Zapatista troubles would be all over and within a year the Mexican would receive justice the same as the citizen of the U.S. receives in his own country. This remark can hardly be appreciated unless the conditions which surround the Mexican Courts are understood.

The middle or lower class of Mexicans are arrested on some trivial matter and thrown into jail, where they stay for six months or a year without trial, so the President's remark meant a great step in the advance of justice.

A federal election had just been held, and, for the first time in the history of Mexico, every citizen had the privilege of casting his ballot. Heretofore the ballot was cast by a few politicians for the whole voting population. It was very noticeable that the middle and lower classes took a serious view of their responsibilities, and the election passed off very orderly.

The higher classes, in many instances, held aloof from voting with the lower classes and, with the usual Mexican foresight, did not realize until it was too late that they had handed the reins of government over to the middle and lower classes, with the result that strong arm rulers with long experience in governing the Mexican people were replaced with inexperienced rulers, who were honest enough in their purpose to lift the lower classes, yet lacked the experience and especially the decision and firmness necessary to hold down the class of Mexicans that take "liberty" for license to plunder to kill.

An incident of my own experience that happened about ten days ago will illustrate this point.

From the mine which I am developing, situated about twenty miles south of Guanajuato, word was received about noon from the mine superintendent that 100 bandits were looting the mining village just below the mine and he expected that they would be at the mine in a few minutes. This was all he had time to say. The Governor's office was immediately notified of the attack by the bandits and they promised to inform the commander of the troops immediately.

In the course of an hour, about twenty-five mounted troops, with a Captain and Lieutenant, started for the mine at a pace that indicated that they did not want to reach the mine before the bandits got through looting and out of reach. The trip to the mine is ordinarily made on horseback in four or five hours. When the troops got about eight miles out, the Captain said that this looked dangerous, and, with half of the soldiers as a body-guard, returned to Guanajuato. The

Lieutenant continued with the rest of the troops until they came to a ranch with a high stone wall enclosing the corral, where they camped for the night. About dark word was brought to the Lieutenant that the band which did the looting was within a mile of his camp and asked him to go after them. The Lieutenant replied that he was told to go to the mine and would not run the risk of encountering any bandits on the way; so he and his troopers remained safely inside of the high stone wall corral until morning, then bravely returned to Guanajuato, without even going to the mine.

This is typical of most of the acts of the soldiers in attempting to hunt down bandits. The soldiers themselves may not be so much to blame, as they have no experience, but the officers have no initiative whatever. They always act on the defensive and will not attack an enemy unless everything is in their favor.

There are fifteen hundred soldiers at different points in the State of Guanajuato; and I know that one hundred Northwestern Mounted Police of Canada could clean up the whole State of bandits in thirty days and keep it clean.

A leader of some bandits and a number of his followers came to Salamanca a few days ago and surrendered to the authorities. As soon as it was learned that they were coming in to surrender, a fiesta was held and they were received with open arms, bands of music, etc. Instead of being treated as bandits, they were received as heroes.

The bandits are supposed to be Mexican cowboys and employees of the large ranches.

As an instance of the little importance the authorities attach to these attacks by bandits, although the Governor's office was informed that the bandits were looting the town at 12:30 p.m., at 4:00 p.m. when a call was made on the Governor, he had not yet been informed of the incident, and when told of the attack, he simply threw up his hands and exclaimed: "Oh! what an awful condition the State of Guanajuato is in! Soldiers not paid and no money in the treasury to pay them."

Mexican nature seems the same from pelado up. They have no initiative for acting in emergencies. They simply seem dazed and forget it as soon as possible and never realize that they should get ready for the next emergency.

The greatest drawback in Mexico today is that the President is not supported by the Mexican people. It is common to hear the remark from Mexicans of all classes, that "Madero got into trouble, let him get out of it." Patriotism is a responsibility not yet born in Mexico. Many wealthy Mexicans, when their country got into trouble, took their families and went to the U.S. and Europe and expect to return when the troubles are all over. It is a question if not a good many of the large land owners of the northern part of Mexico would not welcome U.S. intervention, as they have been heard to say, in that case they would get a much higher price for their land.

From my experience, I cannot see that the Mexicans in general show any feeling against the Americans. In conversation recently with two business associates - Americans employing 250 to 500 laborers - engaged in mining and ranching in several States of Mexico, they stated that they could not recall a single remark of an insulting nature from any Mexican during their twenty-five years' residence in Mexico.

The laboring class knows that it is due to the Yankee mine owner and operator that the miner's wages have increased from 100 to 300 percent with better working conditions, in the last twenty years.

Before the Yankee came, the skilled miner received 75¢ Mex. Cy. per day of 12 hours. Now, he receives from $1.50 to $2.50 Mex. Cy. per day with shorter hours and better working conditions.

Not many years ago, I saw miners packing ore on their backs from a depth of 600 ft. to the surface. Today Mexicans operate practically all the electric hoisting engines, the electric power in some instances transmitted nearly 200 miles.

An American, manager of one of the largest mines in the Republic, informed me, two or three days ago, that the efficiency of Mexican mine labor had increased over 100% in the last three years; that the 3300 employees of his Company were producing considerably more than double per day what 3500 men produced three years ago. Five years ago all mining was done by hand labor, it being the unanimous opinion of mine managers then that Mexicans could never operate machine rock drills; but today this foremost mine manager says: "We do no hand work whatever." A transformation in less than five years from unskilled Mexican labor to skilled machine operators.

Most of the great mining proportion in the three great mining camps, Pachuca, Guanajuato and El Oro, in this part of Mexico, have passed to American and English owners. 25,000 to 30,000 miners in these three camps receive their daily pay from American owned and managed mines - 150,000 Mexicans receive their daily bread in these three camps from American pay-rolls. If intervention or any other cause compelled these mines to shut down, a quarter of a million human beings would be on the verge of starvation in one week, besides affecting 20,000 American and English stockholders. Is this not an item to consider in intervention?

Whatever the Mexican laborer has accomplished in the way of progress, it was done surrounded by poverty and conditions of living that a citizen of the U.S. cannot grasp or understand.

I visited an American ranch about a year ago in harvest. The owner was threshing his wheat and selling it from the machine for $1.50 U.S. Cy. per bushel. The 250 laborers received 24¢ a day for 12 hours. Most of them had families. The wheat was being cut by hand sickles. I asked the owner why he did not cut the wheat with a binder like a live Yankee. He replied that the wheat was being cut and shocked for less than the binder twine alone would cost. Under these conditions a human being can only exist, with no hope of bettering his conditions.

The laborer bears an unequal part of the taxes. On this ranch of 10,000 acres, considered one of the best ranches in the republic, there is a small store for the accommodation of the 250 employees. The taxes on the small store are more than the taxes on the 10,000 acre ranch.

The clothing of the laborer is made from thin cotton cloth on which there is a duty of 100%. In Sonora I have paid $12 duty on a cady of matches which cost $2.00 in Brisbee, Arizona, and a cheap blanket costing $2.25 had a duty of $4.00; yet the capitalist brought in his mining supplies at a nominal rate of duty. Fine china ware, plates worth $300 a dozen in New York, pay the same duty as ordinary plates worth $1.50 a dozen, so much per kilo or lb.

Five percent of the population of Mexico own all the land and hold it practically without paying taxes. Less than five percent of the land is under reasonable cultivation.

Two years ago I examined a large ranch in Chihuahua covering 6,000 sq. miles, 3,750,000 acres, as large as Connecticut and Rhode Island. The National Railway runs for 70 miles through this ranch. I saw corn stalks 16 ft. high with two ears of corn grown here. One peach tree, eight years from the seed, was 20 ft. high with spread of branches of 33 ft. and the trunk 3 ft. in circumference. Five crops of alfalfa were grown per year. A large part of the ranch was as fine land as the Sacramento Valley. The ranch was for sale for about $1.00 gold per acre.

The fertile soil here under the tropical sun produces wonderful growth of trees. Two weeks ago I visited a grove of 150,000 Euclayptus trees, the oldest five years old. Nine trees were shown me less than five years old, 70 to 80 ft. high and 14 ins. in diameter at the trunk, grown without irrigation. I have seen Eucalyptus which grew over 30 ft. high in one year under favorable conditions.

I think a great deal of the present trouble in Mexico can be charged indirectly to the indifference of the American and especially of the American government - to their laxness in regard to questions of international importance, especially in their Consular Service. Perhaps I could explain this point in the following way:

For fifteen years the Consular Agency of the United States in Guanajuato was located in our office. There is little or no pay attached to this office and the office became such a nuisance that it was finally kicked out. A Consular Agent is supposed to have his time at the disposal of any and all of his fellow countrymen who happen to come to Mexico, whether on pleasure to see the country or to make an investment of a million dollars in a mine, and this amounts to a very serious inroad on the time of the Consular Agent, for which he receives no compensation whatever. An offer of $100 a month by the American residents of Guanajuato was no inducement whatever to have the Consular Agency return to our office. A successor was finally found who would accept this American honor. At the time the transfer of the Consular Agency was made, an American had been in jail for several months and had not been able to get a trial. Finally, through the intervention of his friends in the States, the Sec'y of State sent a request through the regular channels to the Consular Agent at Guanajuato that this American be tried and either convicted or set free. The request from the Secretary of State was delivered by the Consular Agent to the proper Mexican judge, and the Judge promptly fined him $10 for contempt of Court. The Consular Agent wished the fine to be made on the Consular Agent and not on him personally and so informed the Judge. The Judge sent over the Chief of Police, who took the U.S. Consular Agent's watch and chain for security until the fine was paid. The Consular Agent redeemed his watch by paying $15 in fines. He took the matter up with his superiors, but was advised that as it was a small amount he had better not say much about it.

The Mexican has come to know that the Yankee will always pay a monetary consideration rather than attempt to get any backing from his country.

Another instance of this kind occurred in Pachuca, which was told me by a physician who has resided there for several years.

About two years ago, during the outbreak of the Diaz-Madero trouble, two Americans were killed in Pachuca. One of the Americans was killed by being dragged through the streets of Pachuca with a lariat around his neck. As soon as this Doctor heard of the accident, he went, accompanied by two Mexican Judges, to view the remains. There was no question whatever in their minds as to how the American met his death. There was a large wound under the chin and around the neck where the rope had cut through the skin and into the flesh and the clothes and side of a shoe on one side of the body were all worn off. He showed me a photograph which he took, at the time, of the wound. A short time after, a Mexican physician was called and made out a certificate of death to the effect that the man died of pneumonia. The matter was taken up through the Consular Service of the U.S. but so far, the American who was murdered by the Mexicans, officially died of pneumonia. The other American killed was called to the door of his house and shot. Nothing has ever been done concerning the murder of these two Americans.

Another instance was an American widow had her child injured by the street car in Pachuca, and this Doctor was called to attend the wounded child. He asked her if she had made any complaint through the American Consular Agent for damages, and she said that she had made complaint but that she had taken the matter up through the British Consul, as she knew that there was no use to put it in the hands of the American Consul.

A number of instances of these kinds could be mentioned. They have happened so frequently that the Mexican thinks it is only a question of a little time and the thing will be forgotten.

Most of the Americans who left this part of Mexico have returned, feeling somewhat sheepish for having left.

When the war talk was at its height, several months ago, the laboring men as a class said: "We don't want to fight, we want to work." There is no question about this trouble being brought to a close in a peaceful way if reasonable intelligence is used in dealing with the Mexicans.

Trusting this statement of facts may be of some interest, I remain,

Yours truly,

(signed) M. K. Rodgers

COMPANIA MEXICANA DE PAVIMENTOS DE ASFALTO Y CONTRUCCIONES, S.A.
3a. Calle de San Agustin No. 78. APARTADO No. 1333.
Mexico, D.F. February 24th, 1913.

Hon. Francis G. Newlands,
    United States Senate,
        Washington, D.C.

My dear Senator:

You are without doubt puzzled by the doings of the past three weeks in Mexico. The apparent treachery of General Huerta is something hard for an American to understand. I beg to state that Huerta is a pretty good old boy. He is the one efficient military commander Mexico has today. Taking orders from President Madero to bombard and attack a low building in the heart of a populous city, he was absolutely opposed to the practice and was forced to work under threat of death. He was surrounded in the Palace by a few troops who were faithful to the President, who has been for the last six months non compos mentis. It took him some nine days to get these troops removed from the Palace when he turned the trick, which was the only thing to be done to save the City of Mexico from destruction on which Madero was bent if such destruction should prove necessary for the recapture of the arsenal. General Huerta was as humane as possible in all of his attack, his aim being to shoot away ammunition harmlessly as fast as it arrived but incidently to defend his troops from the shells of the defenders of the arsenal.

Another apparent outrage was the death of Ex-president Madero. I am of the opinion that Madero was killed as is stated by the Government. The Government had promised faithfully all of the diplomatic corps to spare the life of the insane Ex-president, and I verily believe did their best to comply with this promise. To avoid any suspicion Madero was taken with a small guard at night from the Palace to the penitentiary. In all probability the guards had the usual Mexican or I may say Latin orders in case of an attempt at rescue, to kill their prisoners first and then defend themselves from the attacking party. It is absolutely sure that there was a plot to attack them near the Inter-Oceanic Station, as persons nearby heard the shooting. In the exchange of shots Madero was either shot by his guards or accidently by flying bullets.

If, however, the fact be that the Ex-president was killed by Government officials under the application of the "ley fuga", please do not be led astray by the vaporings of well meaning but ignorant Americans who do not understand these things. If such was the case, it is, of course, deplorable, but kindly bear in mind that it was found, when the Madero Government caved in, Madero contemplated a wholesale slaughter of the prominent Mexicans, including de la Barra, Calero, Garcia Granados, Vera Estanol, and in short all of the more intelligent and most useful element of the country. Also bear in mind that Madero had left quite a following in his family of twelve brothers and others who had been paid large amounts of money out of the "fund for pacification of the country", and who naturally desired to continue to enjoy the use of the public treasury without work. These people had already organized two distinct revolutionary foci in different parts of the country and were holding up trains and committing the usual depredations so long as Madero should be held in jail or confined in the insane asylum. This movement would necessarily continue and make impossible or more difficult the restoration of peace in this country for which we are all looking. With Madero out of business, they will dissolve.

To put a man out of the way under these circumstances is, of course, brutal and inexcusable; but if you or the well-meaning but ill-advised people who may complain of such practice had been here in Mexico during that maniac's bombardment, had heard the bullets, helped dress the wounded, fed the hungry and smelt the burning corpses, and realized that the ignorance of this man cost over 3000 lives and untold suffering, and that his remaining alive would lead to the same disaster here or in other points, your and their ideas of the putting out of the way of the one disturbing element would be more like your or their ideas of the killing of Jesse James. The "ley fuga" and the lynch law have a good deal in common. They are brutal and repugnant but they have been necessary in places where things are raw. A few die to save the many.

We Americans, including John Barrett, Lawrence Godkin, and a great many other well-meaning office-men want applied to the Mexican situation the rules of logic and standard of humanity which we learnt at school. Mexico is in the ethical condition of England up to the beginning of the 17th century where men were hanged for stealing sheep and still continued to steal sheep. Porfirio Diaz ruled this country with the noose and the gun just as the English ruled England up to Shakespeare's time. Poor rattle-brained Francisco Madero tried to run Mexico like Switzerland - tried to run a lumber-country district school with kind words - and the end was certain. Huerta will pursue the Diaz method and we may again have peace and a chance to do business.

I am sure you will not make the mistake of taking your advice on things Mexican from meddlers of the John Barrett class, who themselves would resent my criticism of the way they run their own business. The United States of America is altogether too prone to listen to the theorist who is far away from the trouble zone, but who is the least capable of stating what should be done or of criticizing people on the ground.

I repeat, it is my belief that the killing of Francisco Madero was, as is stated by Francisco de la Barra and other honorable gentlemen, a mistake, but even if it is suspected that the "ley fuga" was applied, please bear in mind that you are not dealing with your conditions, but with these conditions, and that criticism emanating from Boston and other provincial settlements is based on gross ignorance of facts and of conditions of moral development.

In the meantime it would be a great thing if you could lift your voice in the United States now to warn people of our country against listening to ignorant but well-meaning people on grave matters of international importance when the same people of the United States would disregard the advice of an attorney in a case of appendicitis and would spurn the advice of a physician in a problem of bridge building.

Wishing you a continuance of your prominent success, I am,

Yours most sincerely,

(signed) H. Walker.

February 24th, 1913

Hon. Francis G. Newlands,
    United States Senate,
        Washington, D.C.

My dear Senator Newlands:

You see by now what has happened in connection with Mexico during the bombardment. We suffered for ten days in which we all got well accustomed to the sound of the shells and bullets and the smell of burning corpses. I sent Alonsita and Marjorie Fisher to Veracruz, where they had an uncomfortable but less nervous time than they would have had remaining here.

The bombardment of the arsenal in the center of this city of 400,000 inhabitants was the work of a mad-man for the benefit of his own immediate family. It was not alone a bombardment, as the streets especially near the Embassy were held by advance guards of both armies fighting with machine guns, rifles and carbines, and a large number of Americans were wounded besides the four who were killed.

I can say with due conservatism that the only steps taken in all those ten days toward the amelioration of the frightful conditions, cessation of firing or final ending of the matter were made by or through our good Ambassador Henry Lane Wilson, about whom you asked me and about whom, you will remember, I said I have not sufficient words to express his capacity, genius and adequacy for the position.

You probably know that the Embassy was turned into a relief station for the families which were taken out of the danger zone by volunteer Americans in automobiles under the direction of the Ambassador, and from there distributed to houses furnished by other Americans and Mexican families in the supposedly safe district.

Volunteer American drivers and messengers went through the fire three or five times every day carrying official and private cables to and from the cable office. This corps deserves unending commendation for their coolness and bravery. At the Embassy also was a hospital at which combatants and non-combatants were treated irrespectively of Nationality. Had not the fighting stopped on the 18th, the 19th would have seen a newspaper published from the American Embassy giving us all news of the outside world and of the real progress of events in the City, as, of course, all newspapers were suppressed or the offices destroyed by the shell fire.

Mr. Wilson procured a truce to be established on Sunday, which lasted long enough to enable us to relieve some of the families which were in the zone of heavy cannon firing who had been without food or water for some days. He went in automobile directly through the lines of fire four times to the Palace, to see Madero and to the Citadel to see Felix Diaz. His nerve is unquestioned.

During the course of the bombardment Mr. Lascurain, Madero's Secretary of Relations, came to the Embassy and told the Ambassador that a temporary Embassy would be supplied by the Government in a suburb to which he could withdraw, as they must needs make an attack on the arsenal with cannon from the Embassy district which would necessarily draw the fire of the arsenal's big guns in that direction. Mr. Wilson forcefully replied to Mr. Lascurain that the American Embassy would stay exactly where it was, as the opening of the fire in that direction would necessarily draw the fire of the arsenal toward that district in which the majority of the American refugees had assembled.

When the maniac President had finally been put in irons by his outraged soldiers and a conference was necessary between Gen. Huerta and Gen. Diaz, the Ambassador brought them together and each refused to meet the other at any point in Mexico except in the American Embassy and in the presence of Ambassador Wilson. At the conference, due to the genius and ability of Ambassador Wilson, an arrangement was come to which probably means the salvation of Mexico and which put an end to the needless loss of life and property in this Capital. There were a great many details all to the absolute credit of the American Ambassador which I will some day tell you orally, but which necessarily must be omitted from a letter.

Day-before-yesterday sixty members of the English Colony, or probably two-thirds of that colony now in the City, united in presenting to Ambassador Wilson a memorial lauding his attitude, his activity and his work. They paid no such compliment to their own Minister. The American Colony today or tomorrow will do the same thing.

No representative of the United States of America ever acquitted himself in such an emergency - for I verily believe such an emergency never arose - with the credit with which Ambassador Wilson acquitted himself. He is today the biggest power in the Republic of Mexico. Friends of Madero and Government officials came to him seeking his advice which they follow minutely. The United States of America is stronger today in Mexico than it ever has been before, all due to the personality and the acts of Mr. Henry Lane Wilson.

You are a Democrat. Had I voted this year, I would have voted for Woodrow Wilson; although my state being Vermont, I am, of course, congenitally a Republican. Probably a great many people and possibly some friends of yours may be looking for a position of American Ambassador in Mexico this year. The removal of Henry Lane Wilson as American Ambassador and his substitution by any other man in the United States for political reasons would be deplorable, un-American and next to criminal; for it will take a new man at least five years to even understand the situation as it is understood by Mr. Henry Lane Wilson. If Mr. Wilson is substituted by anybody for political reasons, I and most of the Americans resident in Mexico, only one of whom is an employee of the Standard Oil and less than three hundred of whom are employees of the Guggenheims, will consider changing our citizenship.

I realize the exigencies of politics and the need of rewarding political workers, but I feel sure that you, knowing the circumstances, will throw your influence toward the retention of Mr. Wilson in a post in which he better than anybody else can serve the United States Government and add to the prestige which he himself has already built up for it.

Anything that you can do toward the retention of Mr. Wilson or the muzzling of Mr. John Barrett, in spite of whose ignorant and officious published statement, the American Ambassador brought this situation out of chaos into order, will be very much appreciated, not only by myself but by all members of the American Colony in Mexico who, let me add, are a pretty decent group of people doing for the United States what young men are educated in Germany to do for the fatherland.

With kind regards to Mrs. Newlands, I am,

                               Yours most sincerely,

                               (signed) H.W.
                               (H. Walker)

T E L E G R A M   R E C E I V E D
****
From
Frontera, Mexico
Dated June 25, 1913
Rec'd 8:18 A.M. 26th.

Mexico, D.F., March 1st, 1913.

Hon. Gilbert Hitchcock,
      United States Senate,
            Washington, D.C.

My dear Senator Hitchcock:

I am sending you a few photographs of the recent bombardment in Mexico City. Let me assure you that the pictures do not overdraw the horrors of the ten days through which we passed, safely, thanks to nobody but Mr. Henry Lane Wilson. The noise of the cannonading ordered by the maniac head of the constituted government was the worst any of us had ever experienced, and some of us had lived next to the New York elevated railway. There were four Americans killed, and about twenty wounded, who were, with other wounded of all nations, cared for by the nerve and foresight of our Ambassador, and by American boys running automobiles under the American flag -- for the madman had ordered his soldiers to fire on the Red and White crosses, which had refused to carry ammunition for his troops. The contending forces were distributed all over the town, going at it in mutual self-defense with shrapnel, machine guns, rifles and carbines. Even the armistice arranged for Sunday by Mr. Wilson was unable to stop them, for if they did not shoot, they would be shot. Probably 3000 people lost their lives.

I'm not writing this to tell you what we went through. It was bad enough, and we are prepared to go through it again, if that man Barrett is not shut up; but I do want to tell you, as a member of the

Committee on Foreign affairs, the danger to all people in Latin American countries, arising from the fact that our United States of America not only allow ignorant well-meaning people like Barrett to talk, but actually listen to them and take their advice on subjects of which they are ignorant in the most dangerous way -- half-ignorant, and filled up with the mendacity of sweet-scented diplomats, sent to Washington for the purpose of misrepresenting situations, only one of whom, Manuel Calero, has had the honesty to resign and refuse to lie further, and expose the whole scheme in his own Senate.

I will also say, that the American Colony in Mexico City is a pretty decent group of men. The idea is abroad in the United States that we are crooks or employees of the Standard Oil Co. or of the Guggenheims. There is just one of us 24,000 men who is paid by the S.O., and he measures tankers in Tampico. Of the total, less than 300 work for the Guggenheims. The rest of us are on our own hook, in mining, ranching, manufacturing, or in general doing for the United States what young Germans are educated and encouraged to do for their Fatherland. We have spread American manufactures pretty well around, these countries, and, I may say, by knowing and making friends with, and keeping friendly with these people, we are doing a whole lot more for the ends pursued by Mr. Barrett than his whole beautiful organization that Mr. Barrett deserves credit for building up.

Mr. Barrett should be encouraged with his peaceful work. He does not know too much about these countries, as is proved by his idea of a boycott in case of intervention, and of the perils and expense of such an adventure. I may say on the side that he is somewhat of a joke among our Central American friends, who consider him "easy". But I submit, and every American here agrees with me, that when the bullets are flying and the buildings are falling, and men are shooting each other in self-defense, this man has no right or business to interfere with our well-posted representatives on the ground, who know just what they are doing, and just what arguments will reach the sane or insane persons who are responsible for breaches of the civilized code.

Now please look at some of these photographs. They were all taken after the fighting had been going on for at least five days, and after

the corpses had been burned in piles. See the little boy with his chest
blown out. See the good Mexican woman -- the women are the heroes of
this country -- staunching the blood coming from the neck of her man.
See the burning corpses of poor ignorant victims of a madman's caprice,
put into the army from the police station and made to fight on
whichever side their officers happened to be. See the machine guns set
low on street corners, and the men behind log barricades in the middle
of our streets (all of these men were killed). What did John Barrett
know about these things? Our Ambassador was taking the only method
possible to stop these horrors, and was getting results fast. He knows
what he is doing. John Barrett knew what a lot of diplomats had told
him. The thing was about over on the 13th, thanks to Mr. Wilson's
nervy trips to the National Palace, and the strong representations he
made. Then on the 14th, appears in the papers the proud plan of Mr.
John Barrett, looking to stop this killing three thousand miles away, by
the appointment of four men who know as little about it as he -- and
that's the superlative of ignorance -- and whose decision would be
resented and disregarded at best. His blast gave new heart to the
battered government, and they went at it again, and more people were
killed. The pictures show you the killed after Barrett's well-meaning
but fatal publication. I hate to say he killed these people, but his
words spoiled the game Wilson was playing, and the fool who rocks the
boat is as dangerous to society as the robber who shoots into a crowd.

If Henry Lane Wilson had been supported and upheld and let alone
by ignorant publicists, the death rate would have been lower for those
ten days, and the ten days would have been cut to four.

In the United States there is to be a new deal from a clean deck.
There are men with political ambitions who want this job in Mexico. I
send herewith a copy of a resolution passed last night by the American
Colony, regarding the Ambassador and his good wife, and of a speech
made by a decent Englishman at the meeting. Please read these, and
remember what they say, for it's all true. And furthermore, please bear
in mind that Wilson has been through the mill, and knows more valuable
secrets useful in securing peace and settling differences between the
political factions in Mexico than a new man can get in five years, and

that today he is the one man in the country that all factions come to, and refer their differences to, and abide by his decision. Then bear in mind that men of his insight and nerve and acumen are scarce, even in the Democratic Party, and give us a show by working to have him retained at the post wherein he can serve his country better than any other man.

On the general subject of Mexican relations, I can say that we in Mexico are just as opposed to intervention as is Mr. John Barrett, though for different reasons. We feel, not that intervention would lose us our trade, or cost thousands of lives, for it would have no such result. Those are the base grounds on which Messrs. Barrett and Sulzer put their objections. We object, first, because we have been pretty well treated here, and we object to the destructions of an interesting if turbulent nationality, because until the real reason comes, it isn't justified; and even when the real and valid reason for intervention comes we look at intervention with awe, for the simple reason that in the big debating society known as the United States of America, men like Barrett and Sulzer are permitted to lift their voices and ball things up. We foresee that several methods must be applied in dealing with this population, which Mr. Barrett doesn't know anything about. We remember how Edwin Atkinson and Lawrence Godkin and others persuaded McKinley to give that order about pursuing a conciliatory policy at a time when twenty hours more of pursuit would have annihilated all of Aguinaldo's army and ammunition, and organization, and how the two inactive months that followed were sufficient to let Aguinaldo get his courage back and reorganize, and how there were 2000 husky boys from the Middle West buried out there during the four years' war that ought to have been finished in four days, and that the troublemakers from Boston walked the streets free and safe, and were praised for their humanitarian views! We remember Roaring Jake Smith and how these same well-meaning people ruined him for doing his duty. We know that in case of intervention a lot of harsh things would have to be done, and that every one of them would mean the breaking of some dutiful officer of the army or constabulary, at the behest of these ignorant well-meaning theorists three thousand miles away, safe from bullets shot in Mexico and unfortunately safe from violence of an outraged soldiery. We are a lot more opposed to intervention than Barrett is, believe me. We know something about things as they are and Barrett is worried about things as they would not be. We know that Barrett and his like would make peace in Mexico impossible.

This man Barrett and the rest of the kind persons that have pursued his tactics have done more to provoke intervention than anyone else, as a matter of fact. What ever makes the United States go to war? What ever did? "Remember the Alamo". "Remember Fort Sumpter", "Remember the Maine". It wasn't the Interests, or the Trusts or the President, or any of the personalities that Barrett attacks. No. It was always some outrage, and a cry for vengeance, and that is the only thing that will bring trouble with Mexico. Ambassador Wilson and all of us have feared the massacre of men or the raping of women that will cause the cry "Remember". He has striven to make murder of Americans here a dangerous habit. The fact is that during the Madero regime over fifty of us have been assassinated, and nobody has been punished. Nobody has even been brought to trial. It is no fault of Henry Lane Wilson that killing of Americans was becoming so safe an occupation as to invite a general slaughter, but John Barrett, with his statements and his assurances that nothing is going to happen to the Madero Government if it keeps this condition alive was contributing to the likelihood of the outrage we all feared. The Mexicans were whistling in the dark, the same tune that Barrett sung out loud -- that the United States was afraid of them and of the results of intervention, and when they saw the same theories advanced by the President of the Pan American Union, they of course believe them to be true. Every time he lifted his bass voice, he spoiled the long-headed game that Henry Lane Wilson was playing, to the end of protecting us and our families and getting the United States respected, where it is really despised for the reason that the Barretts and the Godkins are allowed to cancel the steps taken by knowing people to build up respect.

In the United States, we don't consult a veterinary on problems of railway construction, nor yet a music master in a case of illness. In the

United States we have a school house on every hill. But in the United States, we listen to the advice of absolutely ignorant people on delicate and deadly questions of foreign policy, where the keenest intimate contact is needed for a realization of the problem. Can you explain it? We can't.

In times of peace, the Barretts and the Godkins and the rest of the Boston community have just as much right to discuss questions of humanity and broad policy and statesmanship as any ignorant people have. They do a lot of good at such times. William Lloyd Garrison didn't know any too much about the thick-lipped negro, but his peacetime talks did a lot of good. Lawrence Godkin runs a sane and helpful newspaper. John Barrett runs a shop where diplomatic flub-dub is answered in kind, and where persons desiring to extend their businesses can get good information, although their representatives sent to these countries are considered vitiated exiles and Standard Oil servants by people at home. But please do, my dear Senator, do something to assure us that during the coming administration the Man on The Ground will be upheld in times of disturbance, and the Man Three Thousand Miles away will not be allowed to mess things up. Look again at these photographs, and then think what ignorant meddling has to answer for.

Wishing you a continuation of your success, I am,

Yours sincerely,

H. Walker

Please don't quote my name.

My dear Senator Newlands:

I don't want to get mixed up in this thing, but being on the ground can assure you that some congressional action looking to the quieting of well-meaning people in times of stress is absolutely essential. For instance, Mr. Barrett ought to be held down to his work, and not allowed to interfere with that of people sent out and paid by the Government to be intimately posted on matters concerning their Government and the safety of its people. The fact is, Madero was insane, and those around him were looking for good excuses to stop that outrageous bombardment. Wilson was playing it that way. Taft's good-natured answer to his crazy telegram was most inopportune. Henry Lane Wilson was getting this thing stopped, but he reminded me of a big guard in a game we played with Holy Cross who grabbed his leg and yelled "Me own man bit me!" For the sake of our families here and for American prestige south of the Rio Grande, please get this little hustling nervy long-headed Wilson kept right here. If he goes, my family returns to the United States forthwith, for a new man will be deceived and worked something awful, I don't care who he is.

Yours sincerely,

(signed) H. Walker

AMERICAN CONSULATE
DURANGO, MEXICO
April 1913.

SUBJECT: Narrative of Political Events,
                Durango Consular District.

THE HONORABLE
      THE SECRETARY OF STATE,
            WASHINGTON.

SIR:

On account of the continued interruption of train and mail service
and the consequent impossibility of reporting opportunely the political
events of significance, I have deemed it best to record such events day
by day as they occur in the form of a diary, which will be forwarded
to the Department as soon as train service resumes.

April 14.

As reported in my despatch No. 238 of April 12, the city of
Durango is now to all intents and purposes in state of siege. The
rebels commanded by Orestes Pereyra, Calixto Contreras and others are
closing in on the city from the east and southeast and are already in
possession of several nearby ranches within sight of this city. The
rebel bands which recently captured Canatlan and Santiage Papasquiaro
and which have been plundering and destroying along the Tepehuanes
branch railroad are now reported to be moving on this city, 1000
strong, from the north. [Portions illegible.]

April 15.

As an illustration of how closely this city is surrounded by
revolutionists, an American citizen started yesterday morning on

horseback for his ranch at Cacaria, Durango. Arrived at Morcillo ranch, only six miles north of this city, he was seized by a small band of revolutionists and thence was conducted to La Labor de Guadalupe, a ranch property 12 miles northeast of Durango City, where Calixto Contreras and Orestes Pereyra with the main body of the rebels are now making their headquarters. The American, Mr. Edwin Halgrimson, was treated with entire courtesy, being only relieved of an American saddle which suited the fancy of one of the rebels. After passing the night in the rebel camp, he was allowed to return to Durango. The rebel chieftains claimed to him to have fully 4000 well armed men, but from his observations he is convinced that there will not be more than half that number. They openly boasted to him that they would be in possession of the city of Durango within a few days.

Word has been received in this city that two or three hundred rebels have put in an appearance about 50 miles to the west of this city along the Chico river. The usual depredations have been committed on the nearby ranches; several railroad bridges have been destroyed; and the extensive lumber camps of the Compania Maderera de la Sierra were visited and robbed of large quantities of merchandise, cash, rifles, saddles and mules. As a direct result, the large saw mill, planning mill and box factory located in this city was today compelled to cease operations, thus throwing out of employment about 75 Americans and more than 1000 Mexicans. This in itself is most serious, as many of the idle men may be induced to enter the revolutionary ranks. Notwithstanding the present policy of the Government to retain all troops in this city for its protection, I have succeeded in inducing him to send out 75 rurales into that section to at least cover the retreat of the American employees to this city.

Another force of 200 rebels has just taken possession of a ranch a few miles south of the city, so that Durango is now rather effectually surrounded on all sides by rebel forces and to all intents and purposes is in state of siege.

April 17.

A monster mass meeting was held last night in the Victoria theater in support of the actual Government, which was attended by the best people of the city. The danger to this city was considered real and when volunteers for its defence were called for, more than 500 responded. No similar procedure has been known in the last three years of revolution and conclusively shows that the better elements are still heartily with the Huerta administration. These volunteers are to be furnished with arms and ammunition and are to be drilled by federal officers. This swells Durango's available fighting force to 1200, which is deemed sufficient to repel any attack on the part of the rebel hordes now surrounding the city. In addition to the forts being constructed at various strategic points on the outskirts of this city, the Government is now erecting barricades of barbed wire across the entrance of several of the most important thoroughfares leading into the city, which will be especially effective in preventing the entrance of horsemen.

A few days ago Carlos Saravia, son of a former Governor of this State and a member of a prominent Durango family, was arrested for suspected complicity with the rebels on the outside. Yesterday, the constitutionally elected Governor, Carlos Patoni who recently obtained under pressure a four months leave of absence from the State Legislature, called upon the present incumbent, Jesus Perea, and demanded the immediate release of young Saravia. Senor Perea replied that the proof was conclusive against Saravia and absolutely refused to consider his release. Whereupon Senor Patoni demanded that he turn back the Government to him. This also Perea peremptorily refused to do without express orders from the Central Government. The federal troops are behind Perea and it is thought that he will be able to hold his own. This incident is related at this time as it may possibly be fraught with serious consequences in the future.

April 18.

The following circular showing that the danger of this city is considered real has been issued by the Committee of social defence, under the caption "To Arms, Citizens of Durango".

"The Committee organized for the social defence issues a call to all the inhabitants of this city, without distinction of class, in order that uniting in a general movement they may hasten to the defence of their homes, menaced by the numerous hordes of bandits which now surround the city for the purpose of sacking it. The Committee appeals to all honorable men in order that they may cooperate, each according to his ability, but all united by a sentiment of solidarity and fraternity to make ourselves respected and to not permit ourselves to be trampled upon by the stolen horses which the rebels are riding. It is urgently requested that every good citizen be present today at three o'clock in the afternoon in the barracks of the 14th regiment in order to complete the proper organization of this corps".

Many new recruits were added to our volunteer force by this meeting at the barracks, the total number being now approximately 500. Those who were without arms and ammunition were supplied with them by the Government and have entered at once upon their duties of patrolling the streets and approaches to this city. Inasmuch as the volunteers have been recruited largely from the most influencial families in the city, it is thought that the moral effect, at least, will be excellent in preventing disturbances on the part of the lower elements within the city.

The rebel hordes without are constantly drawing the cordon closer about the city. Word has just been received that the main rebel force under Pereyra and Contreras is now making its headquarters at La Tinaja ranch, only about 5 miles northeast from Durango. Another rebel force of several hundred occupied yesterday the Ayala ranch about 6 miles southeast from the city. Many other nearby ranches on all sides and practically within sight of the city are serving as depots of supplies for other rebel bands of varying sizes. An attack upon the city is daily expected, but it is not believed that the rebel hordes will be able to effect entry provided there is no treachery among the defenders. Every day during the past two weeks we have had the encouraging news that re-enforcements were on their way to this city from Mexico and other points, but as yet none have arrived.

April 19.

Two rather embarrassing questions for the Americans resident in this city arose yesterday:

First: The Committee composed of representative citizens charged with recruiting volunteer forces for the defence of this city called at this consulate and invited American citizens, if they so desired, to take part in the policing and defence of this city. Later in the day, the Governor of this State made a similar request. Both the Governor and the Committee were informed that in consonance with the principles of International Law and with the explicit instructions from my Government, American citizens must observe the strictest neutrality and not interfere any way between contending forces. They took pains to point out, however, that the undisciplined hordes now surrounding this city should not be dignified by the name of revolutionists, since they were fighting for no definite political principles and that their only object in effecting entry into this city is for the purpose of pillage, destruction and rapine. They added that inasmuch as the foreigners domiciled in this city enjoyed all the rights and privileges in common with Mexican citizens and as their lives and property were equally menaced by the rebels without and the rabble within that it would seemingly be most appropriate for foreigners to join in the defence of the city which would be synonymous with the defence of their own lives and property. Although many of the acts recently perpetrated by the rebels are of a nature to make the average bandit blush for shame, still the fact remains that these rebel hordes are today in possession of by far the greater portion of the State of Durango and claim to be fighting for the re-establishment of the Madero regime, for which reasons they will doubtless have to be considered as a political faction. But under the circumstances and as a mark of courtesy to the Governor and the Committee of Prominent Citizens, I deemed it best to obtain special instructions from the Department covering this particular case, and in this sense I telegraphed the Department last night (see my telegram of April 18, 9 P.M.)

Second: The Governor then informed me that the volunteer forces recruited for the defence of the city were short of arms and ammunition and requested a temporary loan of some of the rifles recently sent by the United States Government to the American Colony in this city. This request I politely refused, stating that the rifles in question had all been sold to American citizens and had therefore passed beyond my control. I also translated for his information a portion of the instructions from the Department of War in connection with the shipment of arms in order to show him that American citizens in their private capacity could not make the loan.

April 20.

All traffic has ceased over the Llano Grande branch railroad which runs westward from this city into rich mountain timber belts. A log train coming from Llano Grande with several Americans and Mexicans on board was fired upon yesterday afternoon by a band of 70 rebels near Garita ranch, only about 4 miles distant from Durango City. Two Mexicans were slightly injured; the Americans escaped unhurt, but were held prisoners for several hours, after which they were allowed to proceed to Durango on foot. The train was burned by the rebels and a considerable portion of track has been torn up, so that traffic has been suspended indefinitely and Durango's large lumber plant has no hope of an early resumption of operations.

The destruction of nearby ranch property by the rebels continues without the least check or hindrance. The sum total of the losses sustained during the last few weeks within a radius of 50 miles of this city will amount of many millions of dollars. Mr. Lawrence V. Elder, the American manager of Ayala Hacienda, less than four miles distant from this city, informs me that the losses caused by the various bands of revolutionists which have been making his place their headquarters for some time will amount to 30,000 dollars.

At about 5 o'clock this afternoon our last telegraph communication with the outside world was severed. For some time past Durango has had only one line of communication, viz: westward across the mountains to Mazatlan and thence to Mexico City. This was the line that was cut yesterday afternoon by newly recruited rebels operating in the western section of the State. Thus the city of Durango is now entirely without rail, telegraph and mail service and is in complete state of siege.

April 22.

An American who reached this city last night after passing through the rebel lines reports that the principal rebel chieftains with the main body of the revolutionary forces are now encamped at San Ignacio ranch about three miles northeast of this city. He was treated with entire courtesy and states that the main rebel leaders, Calixto Contreras, Orestes Pereyra, Mariano Arrieta, Domingo Arrieta and Matias Pasuengo were holding a lengthy conference yesterday afternoon as to the best means of attacking this city. He estimates that there are fully 1500 well armed and equipped men in San Ignacio; t'ere is probably an equal number stationed at other nearby points, forming a more or less complete circle about the city. Mr. Aguirre, the American referred to, brought with him a copy of a recent proclamation issued by the rebel chieftains which makes very curious reading. Articles one and two thereof follow, in translation:

1.   "Before entering the city of Durango it is made known to all the troop in general that the entry into stores or private houses for the purpose of sacking, collecting arms, munitions, horses and saddles is absolutely prohibited." (The fearful destruction and havoc wrought on nearby ranches by the so called liberators bear mute testimony to the successful carrying out of this clause and to what may be expected should this rebel horde enter Durango).

2.   "When the forces of the restoration shall have entered the city of Durango, the leaders of the movement will proceed at once to collecting a forced loan of money sufficient to pay the troops and to defray the other expenses which the war demands."

After the conference above referred to, the revolutionary leaders again demanded of the Governor that he surrender the town immediately. It was confidently believed that the rebels would make an attack upon the city during the night, so all the available troops were stationed at the forts and other strategic points guarding the approaches to the city, while the citizens' volunteer force patrolled the streets throughout the night to prevent possible trouble within the city itself. The night passed, however, without anything out of the ordinary occurring.

A train consisting of 17 cars loaded with logs destined to the Lumber Company in the city was burned yesterday by a small band of revolutionists at a point 25 miles west of this city on the Llano Grande railroad. The American railroad men in charge of the train were allowed to proceed to this city without injury. Word has also just been received that the rurales recently sent out to protect the mountain lumber camps of the Compania Maderera de la Sierra of this city (see page 4) have revolted against the Government, killing two of their officers, and have joined the rebel bands operating in that vicinity.

April 23.

As an aftermath of the Governor's request and my refusal of a temporary loan of the arms and ammunition sent by the United States Government for the protection of the local American Colony (See page 8 of this narrative), the Criterio, a local newspaper of wide circulation, printed the following article in its issue of yesterday:

> "The American Consul in this city in his constant desire for peace and order and in order to aid in the reestablishment of such important and necessary conditions, has offered to furnish to the Supreme Government of the State for the better organization and equipment of the Volunteer Corps a considerable quantity of arms and ammunition which he had in deposit for the defense of American citizens and their interests. The Government accepted this timely aid in the moment in which such munitions were becoming scarce. We congratulate the American Consul for his conduct, which, from every standpoint is praiseworthy and worthy of imitation."

Believing that the above article might be extremely prejudicial to Americans and their interests, especially if the rebels enter the city, and might well be considered a departure from the policy of strict neutrality, the following communication has been sent to the local press and given wide circulation:

> "I have read with no little surprise an article in the Criterio of yesterday relative to the American Consul having furnished a considerable quantity of arms and ammunition to the State Government for the equipment of the Corps of Volunteers.
>
> "This report has absolutely no foundation in fact, and if its author had taken the trouble to inquire at either the Government offices or this Consulate, there would have been no occasion for the publication of this unfortunate error.
>
> "Trusting that, in the interest of veracity, you will have the kindness to insert the foregoing in your issue of today.
>
> Yours very truly".

The Governor also agreed of his own volition to officially deny the Criterio's erroneous statement. The offical denial appeared in Periodico Oficial of April 24, 1913.

The Government troops and the citizens' volunteer forces have been called out many times during the day on the rumor that the rebels had begun the attack at widely separated points, but in each case the report has proven false. The garrisons have been heavily strengthened at all outposts during the day and all is in readiness for the momentarily expected attack. For the better understanding of the events which follow, I am attaching hereto (Enclosure No. 1) a map of the city of Durango, on which I have indicated with squares of red ink the several forts which have been erected to guard the approaches to the city. For convenience, these forts have been numbered beginning at the northwest corner and continuing north, east, south and west, from one to 16.

The long expected attack upon this city began yesterday afternoon at about 4 o'clock, a considerable detachment of rebels having taken possession of the Cerro Mercado (Iron Mountain) to the north of the city (indicated on the attached map by a capital "A), whence they opened fire upon the Government forces stationed on the Cerro de Guadalupe (Fort No. 2 on the attached map). Several thousand shots were exchanged between the two contending forces from that time until dark at a range of practically one mile. Two of the defending force were wounded; the rebel casualties are unknown.

Some desultory firing took place during the night at many widely separated points around the city, which indicated that the rebels were occupying vantage points for a general early morning attack. At daybreak this morning the firing was resumed, the city being attacked from all four sides simultaneously. The main rebel forces were, however, massed to the east of this city, where the battle raged most furiously. At a little before 6 o'clock in the morning, the rebels surrounded and took by assault Fort Zatarain (Marked No. 8 on enclosure No. 1) few of the garrison of 25 Government troops escaped. A force of 60 federal cavalry were at once despatched and by a brilliant sally succeeded in recapturing the fort, some 20 of the rebels being captured and executed on the spot.

It was discovered in the early morning hours that several Maderista partisans had taken position on the house tops, whence they were firing into the volunteer forces which patrolled the streets. Some 25 or 30 of these assassins had fortified themselves in a large garden on Calle Pila in the eastern part of the city (Marked by a capital B on the attached map). Several of the volunteer forces were killed or wounded, but did most effective work in surrounding and capturing the men responsible for these outrages; the majority of those captured were promptly executed, and in this manner the rear fire was speedily silenced. It is now evident that there was a well defined plot among the Maderista sympathizers within the city to aid the rebels on the outside and by placing the defenders on the outskirts of the city between two fires to render their position untenable. The fact that the city is not in the possession of the rebels at this time is due largely to the most efficient patrol of the streets by the citizens volunteer forces who were able to silence this dangerous back fire.

The city was also heavily attacked from the south during the early morning hours. The rebels gained possession of a large two story house about one kilometer south of forts marked Nos. 14 & 15 on the attached map. A well directed cannon shot from fort 14 passed through the center of the house occupied by the rebels, killing many of them. Taking advantage of the confusion, a cavalry charge was made and some 20 rebels were surrounded, captured and executed. Several assaults were also made from the west against the Cerro de Remedios (Fort No. 16 on the attached map), all of which were repulsed by the federal defenders. To the north of the city desultory fighting continued throughout the day at long range with little damage to either side.

All told, a conservative estimate of the losses of the day would be: 200 rebels, 50 Government troops, 10 citizen non-combatants, and the execution of about 10 or 15 persons engaged in or suspected of being implicated in firing into the government forces from behind. [N.B. later returns indicate that these figures are somewhat exaggerated.] Tonight the advantage lies decidedly with the federal defenders who have succeeded in repelling the rebel attack all along the line.

It has been deemed prudent to take certain preliminary steps looking to the concentration of foreigners in this city in case there should be imminent danger of its falling into the hands of the rebel hordes. The McDonnell Institute, an American college occupying nearly a whole block in the center of the city, has been selected as the site most easy of access and most capable of defence. It has been stocked with provisions and necessary supplies and word has already been given out to foreigners resident in dangerous outlying districts that the Institute is at their disposition.

During the last few days, several Mexican citizens have approached this consulate with a view of obtaining asylum for themselves and their families. In each case, this has been courteously but firmly refused.

April 25.

At daybreak firing was resumed to the north, east and south of the city, the main rebel forces being this time concentrated to the north on and near the Iron Mountain (Marked with a capital "A" on the enclosed map). Early in the day the two federal cannon were trained upon the rebel positions near the Iron Mountain and for several hours kept up a continuous fire. The most of these shots were very well directed and caused considerable losses and no little confusion in the rebel ranks. Taking advantage of this confusion, a series of federal cavalry charges were made which dislodged the rebels from all their important positions and caused them to retreat in wild disorder towards the north and east. The federal pursuit continued to a point about five kilometers north of the city. In addition to the rebels killed, many were made prisoners and afterwards executed; only three of the federals were killed. A portion of the rebel force which retreated northeastward ran right into the column of 400 irregular Government forces under the command of General Cheche Campos which were marching to the relief of this city, at San Ignacio ranch 3 kilometers distant. It is reported that nearly 100 rebels were either killed or taken prisoners in the engagement which followed.

The several rebel attacks made on the city from the east and south were repulsed with ease. The day closed with the rebels completely routed at all points and retreating in considerable disorder from the environs of the city. It is not thought that they will return to renew the attack.

The vanguard of Cheche Campos' irregulars began to arrive in the city early in the afternoon and by nightfall 400 of his troops had been added to the local garrison. These troops in company with about 400 others left Torreon by train more than a week ago, repairing the railroad line as they came. On account of the urgency of the situation, half of the forces (the 400 which have just arrived) detrained at Tapona station, 48 miles distant from this city and made the rest of the journey overland. The remaining 400 are with the repair train slowly working their way into Durango. A repair train will also be sent out from this city tomorrow, so it is hoped that train service will speedily be resumed after an interruption of approximately two months.

April 26.

In the early hours of the morning a few shots were exchanged at long range between retreating bands of rebels and the soldiers garrisoning the forts to the north and west of the city. One federal soldier was wounded; the rebel losses are not thought to have been much greater. The future plans of the rebels are unknown, but they have apparently given up all hope of capturing the city of Durango at the present time. The main revolutionary forces have retreated to the mountainous districts to the north and west of this city to recuperate and lay plans for future action; some smaller bands are still pillaging the rich agricultural sections to the south and east of Durango City. They are doubtless very much embittered at their failure to take this city and will probably wreak their vengeance upon the neighboring small towns and outlying ranches and mining properties. Emilio Campa is only awaiting the arrival of the balance of his irregular forces in order to inaugurate a campaign of extermination calculated to rid the State of these defeated and demoralized rebel bands. It is a striking commentary upon the kaleidoscopic changes in Mexican politics that such rebel and bandit chieftains as Emilio Campa, Cheche Campos, Luis Caro, Escajeda, Zamora, Rodriguez and others, who a few months ago were looting, destroying and committing other outrages in this State, are now at the head of their respective irregular guerrillas fighting for law and order and furnishing protection to the capital of this desolated State. The bandit chieftains of yesterday are the Generals and Colonels of today; our erstwhile defenders are the rebels and bandits which have just been repulsed from this city, and so on ad infinitum.

April 27.

Today was the first day in some time that rifle firing was not heard in the outskirts of the city, the rebels having retired at least beyond range, which is a considerable distance in Mexican warfare. At noon today General Cheche Campos at the head of more than 500 irregular troops (former Orozquista revolutionists) arrived in this city after a hard 10 days journey partly by train and partly overland from Torreon. This swells Durango's effective fighting force to more than 2000 men, as follows: Federals of the line, 300; Durango State troops, 400; irregular troops, recently arrived, 1000; citizens volunteer force, 500.

April 30.

The last few days have produced little material change in the local situation. From information gleaned from travellers, the scattered rebel bands are still on all sides of the city, at a few miles distance; they are still threatening to attack and sack this city, but, after the severe defeat administered, it is not generally believed that they will return to renew the attack. Durango is still completely cut off from railroad and telegraph communication with the outside world. The Government troops still remain inactive in this city, but the Governor informs me that plans are now being perfected for the inauguration of an effective offensive campaign of extermination.

May 1.

Word has just been received in this city that the main rebel bands under Calixto Contreras and Orestes Pereyra are now concentrating in the vicinity of Cararia and Canatlan, some 25 miles to the north of this city. Late last night some 400 of the irregular forces of Cheche Campos were despatched to that section to prevent further concentration. An exploring party of about 100 men was also sent to the west of the city, where it was reported that the rebel bands of the brothers Arrieta and Octaviano Meraz were concentrating. All remains tranquil in this city and its environs.

A translation of the Governor's telegram to President Huerta, dated today, describing the events of the siege is enclosed herewith (Enclosure No. 2).

May 2.

The 400 irregular forces of Cheche Campo's command sent north yesterday encountered the main rebel force near Canatlan, 25 miles north of this city, by whom they were severely defeated, and are now retreating in some disorder to this city. The actual casualties are unknown, but it is known that 17 wounded men were brought back with the retreating troops. More than 1000 revolutionists have now concentrated in the vicinity of Canatlan and this number is constantly being augmented by the arrival of other bands, all of which recently took part in the attack upon Durango. The rebels themselves state that they have by no means abandoned the idea of taking this city and are now only awaiting the arrival of Francisco Villa at the head of 1000 rebels to renew the attack. Villa recently captured the city of Jimenez, Chihuahua, from which he was dislodged a few days later by federal forces. Villa is also said to be bringing a large quantity of ammunition.

Many sensational arrests of prominent citizens of this city, among whom are two former Governors of this State, have been made during the last few days. These men, all of whom are strong Maderista sympathizers, are suspected of furnishing material aid to the revolutionists on the outside and of fomenting a sympathetic movement within the city itself.

May 3.

This afternoon at 4 o'clock the first train reached Durango from Torreon after a continuous interruption of service of more than two months. This train has been slowly working its way into Durango for the past three weeks, practically every bridge between here and Torreon, as well as considerable sections of track, having been destroyed. The arrival of the train was the occasion for much rejoicing in Durango; the train was met by a brass band and a committee of prominent citizens, headed by the Governor of the State. Two hundred federal troops accompanied the repair train and have now been added to our local garrison. Behind the repair train came three freight trains laden with coal, sugar and many other necessities and food stuffs which had become very scarce in Durango during the long period the city has been cut off from the outside world.

The following telegram from the American Consular Agent at Torreon indicates that there has been very little change in conditions in the Laguna district: "Train left here today for Durango. All railroads cut excepting to Mexico City. Many rebels in district, but are committing few depredations". Shortly after the receipt of this message, telegraph communication was again severed.

May 4.

The construction train which has been laboriously working its way for the past few weeks from Torreon to Durango had scarcely more than reached the latter point when word was received that the rebels were again operating along the line of railroad. The rebels commanded by Calixto Contreras and numbering about 600 turned eastward from Canatlan day before yesterday, passed through Avino, where the property of the Avino Mining Company, a British Corporation, was completely sacked and everything of value was either appropriated or destroyed, and thence continued on to Gabriel, a station on the International Railroad 35 miles northeast from this city. From San Gabriel this rebel force turned east along the line of railroad burning bridges and destroying other property as they went. A traveller who has just arrived states that practically all the bridges between the station of Gabriel and Pasaje, a distance of nearly sixty miles, have again been destroyed; the telegraph line which follows the railroad has also been severed at many points. From Pasaje the rebels turned south to Cuencame, the old rendezvous of Contreras' men and where, it is said, that they have a considerable store of ammunition. The rebel forces commanded by Orestes Pereyra, Domingo and Mariano Arrieta are still reported to be spread over the rich agricultural section to the north and east of Canatlan, where they are committing their customary depredations.

A repair train has again been sent out from this city to rebuild the bridges, some of which have been destroyed more than 20 times during the last two years. All of Cheche Campos' irregular force of 800 men have also been sent out to do police duty along the line of railroad in an effort to keep traffic open to Torreon.

A messenger just arrived from Chalchihuites, Zacatecas, brings several letters indicating that the revolutionary movement is rapidly spreading in northern Zacatecas. On April 27, the city of Sombrerete was captured without resistance by 400 rebels under the command of Natera, Cabral and others. A forced loan of ten thousand pesos was raised, but few other depredations were committed. The towns of Sain Alto, Nieves, Mal Paraiso, Jerez and La Noria were subsequently taken by the same rebel force. On May 1 the city of Chalchihuites was entered by a band of 50 outlaws under the leadership of Jose de la Torre. A forced laon of 600 pesos was levied and business and private houses were generally looted.

May 5.

Many disquieting reports of revolutionary activity in the extreme western part of this State, heretofore comparatively free from trouble, are beginning to come in. A messenger just arrived from Basis reports that the Basis Mining Company (a British Corporation) plant and property were completely sacked and the foreigners employed in the mines (3 Englishmen and 1 American) were made prisoners and threatened with death unless four thousand pesos were immediately produced. Not having any such sum of money, bar silver was offered instead, but was indignantly refused by the bandits, who decided to give them until the following morning to produce the required sum. During the night the four men succeeded in evading their guards and escaped on foot. The direction taken by them and their present whereabouts are unknown, but the difficulties encountered will be great as Basis is in the heart of the mountains and fully 5 days distant by mule from either Durango or Mazatlan.

The garrison of 60 State rurales commanded by Octaviano Meraz and stationed at Ventanas, another important mining camp in the western part of the State, recently revolted against the Government and have been spreading desolation in Ventanas and other nearby camps. For nearly two months no word has been received from the American Consular Agent in Topia and it is generally reported that that place as well as several other neighboring camps is now in possession of the rebels.

May 6.

Mezquital, an important town about 40 miles south of this city and the seat of Government of the partido of the same name, was entered day before yesterday by a band of about 100 rebels after a sharp engagement of several hours with the towns people who were defending the place. Business and private houses were sacked and the customary outrages committed.

May 7.

An American citizen who has just reached this city by horseback from Canatlan, 25 miles north of Durango, reports that the entire north country is still swarming with rebels. The 400 revolutionists commanded by the brothers Arrieta are spread over the rich agricultural section north and east of that place and are leaving little of value behind them. The large American ranch at Cacaria owned by the Varn brothers has been repeatedly visited by rebel bands and has lost more than 200 head of cattle, this year's corn crop and much other property.

I have just received a letter from Mr. J. O. Emerson, Manager of the Ventanas Mining Company at Ventanas, Durango, setting forth the conditions of actual anarchy which prevail in the western part of the State, and the many recent desertions of Government troops to the rebel ranks. (See Enclosure No. 3).

May 8.

The construction train which has been repairing the railroad between Durango and Torreon was forced to return to this city tonight on account of increased rebel activity ahead. The construction train brought with it the news of the capture of Velardena, Asarco and Pedricena by the rebels under the command of Calixto Contreras and Orestes Pereyra. The meager details of what occurred have been gleaned from 5 troopers who managed to escape from the Pedricena garrison to the construction train, by which they were conducted into this city. It seems that the rebels first cut telegraph and railway communication between Pedricena and Torreon, so that no assistance could come from that source and then surrounded the federal garrison of 100 men at Pedricena and the 25 in Velardena. The 5 federal troopers who reached the construction train are the only ones known to have escaped. They report that all the officers and many of the men were made prisoners and subsequently shot and that the rebels captured a federal cannon and a large quantity of arms and ammunition. No further information is obtainable concerning the subsequent depredations of the rebels as we are entirely without rail and telegraph communication, but considerable anxiety is felt for the safety of the 50 Americans employed in the mines and smelter of the American Smelting and Refining Company at Velardena and Asarco.

The construction train had repaired the railroad from Durango City to a point beyond Yerbanis, when a considerable body of rebels was seen occupying the heights in front, evidently laying in wait for the approach of the train; this coupled with the arrival of the 5 federal refugees induced them to suspend operations and return to Durango. The 800 irregular troops which had been patrolling the repaired line were also ordered back to Gabriel, 35 miles northeast of this city, to serve as a buffer against the nearer approach of the rebels, so the hope of a speedy resumption of telegraph and train service has been indefinitely deferred. Marshall law again prevails in this city and the authorities are busily engaged in strengthening the fortifications guarding the approaches thereto. The rebels have been openly boasting for some time that they were only awaiting re-enforcements from Chihuahua in order to renew the attack upon this city and recent events seem to lend some color to their statement.

In view of recent alarming events in all sections of this State, a meeting of all foreign consular representatives was held today, at which it was decided to attempt to send a messenger to the nearest telegraph point to inform our respective Governments of the actual state of affairs, thus correcting the erroneous impression of peace and tranquility to be gathered from the Governor's recent official telegram (see enclosure No. 2). The following telegram to the American Embassy was accordingly entrusted to two messengers, one of whom is to make the journey overland to Torreon and the other will attempt to reach Fresnillo, Zacatecas, on the line of the Mexican Central railroad; it is hoped that one or the other of these messengers will succeed in breaking through the blockade:

> "Governor's official report to President number 976 inaccurate. Although besiegers have retired, city is still cut off. All State is now in possession of rebels except capital and large parties again advancing towards capital. Federal ammunition reported short. Urgently request federal reenforcements. This message being sent overland by messenger. All foreign consuls concur. Please inform Spanish, British, German and French ministers. Reply by telegraph American Consular agent Torreon."

The substance of the above message was also sent by the same conveyance to the Department.

May 11.

The irregular force of 100 men commanded by Cheche Campos which had been patrolling the newly repaired railroad between Durango and Pedricena, were ordered back to this city for its protection, reaching here this morning at 9 o'clock. Thus the month's work spent in repairing railroad and telegraph communication to Torreon has gone for naught and the lines are again exposed throughout their entire distance to the caprice of every small band of rebels or robbers. The recall of these irregular forces was due to the fact that the local authorities are expecting another concerted rebel attack in the near future. A complete chain of forts and barricades is being extended around the city; this outer barrier is in turn supported by an interior system of fortifications, the whole leaving the city far better protected than when the rebel attacks of April 24 - 26 were repulsed.

May 12.

The 60 State rurales sent westward to repair the telegraph line to Mazatlan and to again establish communication with the outside world reached Llano Grande, 65 miles west of this city, yesterday. At that point a sharp skirmish occurred with 150 rebels commanded by Lorenzo Mendoza, Sergio Pasuengo and others, in which three of the rebels were killed and the rest forced to retire. The telegraph repair party will continue on westward.

A messenger just arrived from northern Zacatecas reports that the Mexican Central Railway has not been operating north of the city of Zacatecas since May 5th. Thus Torreon, the most important railroad center in the northern part of the Republic, has been completely cut off from communication with the outside world since that date.

May 14.

A chance presents itself to send the foregoing diary of events covering the month from April 14 to May 14 overland to the city of Zacatecas, 200 miles distant, which is now our nearest railroad connection. As this overland route is very precarious, only one copy is sent; the additional copies will be forwarded as soon as mail communication reopens.

I have the honor to be, Sir,
Your obedient servant,

(signed) Theodore C. Hamm,
American Consul.

[Editor's Note: Enclosures listed above not included.]

                    *   *   *   *   *   *   *

                                        Ventanas, (Via Chavarria) Durango,
                                            Mex., May 2, 1913.

T. C. Hamm, Esq.,
    U. S. Consul.
        Durango, Dgo.

Dear Sir:

I beg to advise that I arrived safely at Ventanas, but found enroute that the federal garrison at San Isidro, commanded by Lorenzo Mendoza, had mutinied and started for this place. Not having a competent guide, I was unable to pass them on the road, reaching here one day after they had taken the town by stating that they were federals, entering and disarming the rebels here. Later most of the garrison joined them.

The rebels have now left here for Durango via Pueblo Nuevo. The total value of merchandise, arms, etc. secured from this company and its employees was about $4,000 U. S. Cy. A detailed list of losses by American employees will follow later. No personal indignities were offered to the foreigners, other than a speech to us by Mendoza when leaving, and in a state of intoxication, to the effect that he would like to kill all Americans, as they were "sucking the life-blood of the country", and that he would return later and see to it. I doubt whether he was voicing the general sentiment of the rebels, as no evidences of ill-will on the part of the rest were noted. The troop leaving numbered over 100.

The San Dimas rising was headed by Miguel Laveaga, who is said to be now heading for the coast country with 250 men. He is also said to be coming here. We have had no authentic news from there. Octaviano Meraz escaped to his ranch with ten men, it is said.

Yours very truly,

(signed) J. O. EMERSON.

AMERICAN CONSULATE

Tampico, Mexico
May 25, 1913

SUBJECT: Political Conditions.

THE HONORABLE
     THE SECRETARY OF STATE,
          WASHINGTON.

SIR:

Referring to my despatch No. 727 on the 12th inst., I have the honor to report further in regard to political conditions in this Consular District.

I have since confirmed my statement that no troops were sent either to Ebano, S.L.P. or to Matamoras, as I had been advised. I know of no reason why misleading information should have been given to me or anybody else unless it would be that the authorities had a desire to impress local people with their ability to meet all situations.

It has been since confirmed that the bridge at Taninul was not destroyed by the revolutionists. Traffic was held up for several days but was finally opened by the coming of Federal troops. It was only a short time until traffic was again interrupted. On Sunday, May 18th, the train from Tampico was stopped at Ebano. After robbing the train and the passengers, the alleged revolutionary party robbed the camp of the Mexican Petroleum Company at that place and got a number of guns and a number of horses and saddles; and also about 800 pesos in money. The revolutionary party stayed only a short time. Within an hour after the revolutionists left, a special train of 75 Federals arrived at Ebano.

Traffic was opened on the road and lasted for several days. The communication was again cut on the 22nd inst. It is very difficult to secure reliable information in regard to the condition of the railroad but it is said that several kilometers of track have been torn up and destroyed. It is also stated that no further trains will be run until the government can send troops to protect them.

I am unable to state when this line will be again open for transportation of passengers and mail. In regard to the condition of the railroads it is proper to state that it has been ordered that no freight other than fuel shall be carried on any of the railroad lines until further orders. The object of the government is to carry coal and oil to interior points for the use of the railroads and the large shelters. This order has been modified in order to permit the carrying of food supplies in exceptional cases to points where the military officials see that such action is necessary. As a result, the commerce of this port is at a standstill. The Customs House wharves are congested and the officials have difficulty in finding places for the cargos of incoming ships. If this condition of affairs continues it may become so bad that a number of men will be thrown out of employment and further complicate the local conditions.

Referring again to despatch No. 727, which showed that Tampico was at that time cut off from railroad communication farther north than Victoria as well as to the south, I beg to advise the Department that during the evening of Monday, the 12th, information was received by the officials in this City stating that the train from Victoria to Tampico had been seized by a large band of rebels. The officials feared that the revolutionists would attempt to enter Tampico on this train. They therefore made all necessary military preparations to resist the attack. Soldiers were stationed at the various points of entrance into the City. The draw-bridge above the City was opened in order to prevent any entrance from the south. By order of the Federal officials, a number of rails were removed near Dona Cecilia in order that the train which the rebels were supposed to be coming in on would be derailed. A great number of extra police were sworn in and placed at the police station.

Nothing whatever transpired except that the entire population of the City was greatly excited and confused by these military operations. This was the more so because the same morning a number of pieces of artillery had been placed at the old abandoned fort known as the "Casa Mata".

During the excitement Monday evening the local Postmaster came to me and requested permission to place his money and valuable official papers in the Consulate during the night. I granted his request but would accept no responsibility or give any receipt. All of the matter on deposit with me was returned to him the next morning.

During the same confusion the manager of the Bank of Tamaulipas asked me if it would be possible for him to deposit the funds of the bank, 1,000,000.00 pesos, on board the U. S. Warship "IDAHO", which was in port. I assured him that I thought there was no danger during that evening and promised to give him a reply the next day. After conferring with Capt. Howard, I advised the manager that Capt. Howard was authorized to receive all money, jewels, etc., which would be deposited on board his ship, with the distinct understanding that Capt. Howard would accept no responsibility whatever until the said articles were delivered on board.

During this confusion, the manager of the National Bank stated to me that the time had arrived for several hundred marines to be landed from the U. S. Warship for the protection of the City. I advised Mr. Rodriquez that the U. S. warships were not here to take a part in the war. Furthermore, that they were here simply to protect the interests of Americans, which to me did not appear to be threatened at that time.

The following day, May 13th, there was still a great deal of excitement in the City. The Board of Trade was called together and a commission was appointed for the solicitation of alleged voluntary contributions for the equipment and maintenance of a force of 100 well armed and well mounted men.

In order that the Department may thoroughly understand the situation I have to advise that on Monday afternoon Col. Rivera, Jefe de Armas, during a conversation which I had with him told me that he had just finished a telegraphic conference with Gov. Arguelles, and Gen. Arzamendi. He showed me a telegram which indicated that the municipal authorities had been instructed by the Governor to cooperate with Col. Rivera in the work of re-organizing the police force and in the work of furnishing adequate protection to the City of Tampico. This was the first step toward placing the military authorities in Tampico above the civil. He also showed me another telegram indicating that the local Chamber of Commerce was to be called together and requested to assist in the defense of this City.

The Chamber of Commerce was called together as herein afore stated on May 14th. The merchants were very much excited and thought that something must be done in order to secure adequate protection. They had been impressed by the military precautions which had been taken during the preceding morning when artillery pieces had been placed in the old "Casa Mata". They had been impressed with the fact that Tampico was cut off from all railroad communication with the outside world. They had been very much excited by the proceedings of the authorities during the previous evening. They were still expecting the train from Victoria to arrive in charge of the alleged revolutionary party. All telegraph communication had been cut off.

After the merchants of the Chamber of Commerce were impressed with the situation, the Jefe de Las Armas told them that he was able to defend the City against the revolutionists. If he did not directly so state, the merchants of the Chamber of Commerce understood that he would be unable to protect the City from the possibly dangerous element which exists inside of the City. The merchants were also informed that the sum of 36,000 pesos would be required to equip and maintain an organization of 100 well armed and well mounted men, whose business it would be to protect the City. They were also informed that these men would be under the command of the military commander. They were further informed that at the end of three months the Federal Government, through the Minister of War, would take over this organization. This latter information was confirmed by the receipt of a telegram from the Minister of War.

The local Chamber of Commerce did not care to bear this entire burden alone. It deemed proper that other merchants in the City should also bear a part of this expense. Notices were sent out to a number of merchants saying that they would be visited by a commission the following day. However, the commission did not visit them. The merchants received citations to appear at the City Hall. Upon arrival at the City Hall the merchants were informed of the amount which they were expected to voluntarily contribute.

Practically all the large mercantile houses in this City are owned by foreigners. These foreign merchants were thus summoned and told that they were to contribute a certain amount voluntarily for the equipment and maintenance of this armed force which was to be under the command of the military commander of the City. Under the circumstances, it appeared much easier for these foreign merchants to submit to the demand of these alleged voluntary contributions than to refuse payment of same. They one and all feared that it would cost them more to refuse than to pay.

Some of the American merchants consulted with this Office and were informed that such contributions made by them might be construed as a violation of the strictly neutral standpoint which the United States wishes its citizens to observe. The British Consul, Mr. Hubert W. Wilson, who is the Dean of the Consular Corps, also consulted with this Office in regard to the matter.

As a result of his investigations, the British Consul called a meeting of the entire Consular Corps. In that meeting, which was held in this office, it was unanimously decided that the matter should be taken up with the authorities and that steps be taken for the preservation of neutrality. A meeting with the military commander and the mayor of the City was arranged for the next afternoon. At that conference the military commander and the mayor of the City was arranged for the next afternoon. At that conference the military commander informed the Consular Corps that he was well able to defend the City. That he could see, as called to his attention by the Consular Corps, that such contributions would be a violation to strict neutrality. At this point it was suggested that the matter might be remedied by changing the form of the receipt which was signed and given by the authorities to the contributors. The receipts contained the words "For the Defense of the People." The authorities suggested that the receipts should be made to read "For the Purchase of Necessities for the Municipality. Every member of the Consular Corps, except myself, was satisfied with the change.

It was difficult to see how changing the form of the receipt could change the nature of the transaction. I so explained the matter to the officials and further suggested that it would be well to change the form and nature of the organization which was to be equipped and maintained with this money. After debating the matter for some time the authorities agreed to use this money for the equipment and maintenance of a special police force, a civil rather than a military body. All the police force to be under the control of the municipal authorities rather than the military. It appeared that such contributions to such a civil body could not be construed as a violation of neutrality.

Three things were established by the conference of the Consular Corps; first, that these contributions were to be considered as absolutely voluntary and no merchant was to be prejudiced by refusing to comply with the request that had been urged upon him; second, the form of the receipt was to be changed; and third, the form and nature of the organization was to be changed.

During the meeting it was evident that there was absolutely no necessity for the raising of this fund. It was also evident that the ground was well prepared before the demand was made for these alleged voluntary contributions. It is also certain that the authorities themselves know that this method of raising funds is absolutely irregular.

They stated as much to the Consular Corps with the explanation that it was necessary because the municipal Governor could raise no special fund without the authorization of the State Legislature, which would probably require some two or three months.

I believe that if it was not for the fact that nearly all of the merchants had already paid the amounts requested from them, that the Consular Corps would have taken a more firm stand in the matter and objected to it in its entirety. I think that the authorities and merchants will be more careful in such matters in the future.

Not only did the authorities use existing conditions as a means of extracting money from foreign merchants but they also used them to make the civil authorities more or less subject to the military authorities.

Among other things, a regulation was declared by which it was unlawful for any one to be on the streets after 11:00 o'clock at night without a pass signed by the military commander. This regulation was put into effect without notice of the same being sent to the foreign Consuls. As a result, the Consul Corps was called together by the British Consul and a commission was sent to confer with the authorities, requesting them to advise members of the Consular Corps of such important regulations. This request was granted and I think will be fully complied with in the future.

The number of ways in which the civil authority is gradually made subordinate to the military make a large part of the Mexicans believe that they no longer have guaranties. This opinion has become much stronger during the last few days. This is very largely due to the action of the military authorities in regard to the number of arrests which were made on the charge of conspiracy against the government.

On May 21st ten men were arrested on such charges and were immediately placed on board the Mexian gunboat "Vera Cruz", which was then in port. This action was, it is believed, taken to prevent the service of "Writs of Amparo" or habeas corpus. However, before the men were taken on the gunboat, such writs were served in favor of two of the prisoners. The gunboat left Friday morning to take these prisoners to Vera Cruz, from which point they were to be sent to Mexico City. The authorities claimed to have letters and documents showing that the men who were arrested were in conspiracy with forces outside of the City. It was alleged that the plan was to start a large fire in the center of Tampico on the 25th; it was expected that this fire would draw the attention of the authorities more or less from the entrances of the City. Forces outside of the City were then to attack and in the confusion, the forces inside would be able to hold the balance of power and capture Tampico. It is alleged that these inside forces were promised that they would be given a certain number of hours in which to sack the City.

Experiences show that it is always difficult to form an opinion as to how much confidence can be placed in such charges. Very frequently such charges are made for political or revengeful purposes.

An incident occurred on May 23rd which the authorities claimed justified the arrests which they made as herein before stated. A passenger train was sent out according to custom at 6:00 o'clock in the morning to go to Gonzalez, which is about 20 miles out of the City. This passenger train had no difficulty in going through the yards inside of the municipality; about an hour later a troop train was sent out in the same direction to assist the force which had been repairing the track. This train was derailed near Dona Cecilia within the limits of this municipality. The fireman and two brakemen were killed. Investigation showed that a number of rails had been taken up and replaced without being properly fastened. The work was also concealed by the placing of old grass on the track. It was thought that this work was done by revolutionary sympathizers in that vicinity and it was said that a number of arrests were made. It is not known what became of the men who were arrested and it is thought that they have mysteriously disappeared. This wreck was reported the same day and a troop train sent out in the afternoon. It is stated that about three or four kilometers beyond the point where the wreck occurred in the morning, the force on the train caught a number of men tampering with the track. It is said that all of these men were shot while the soldiers were trying to capture them. It is difficult to obtain authentic information on these points. Such occurrences have created great distrust and great fear in the minds of local people and many of them believe that the government gives no guarantee at present.

The former mayor of this City, Sr. Angel Boeta came to this office last evening and confidentially advised me that he believed that he was in great danger of being arrested on false charges and that he felt that he would have no protection from the Mexico Government. He wanted to know if he could seek protection in this Consulate. The right of asylum was explained to him fully. He was told that this right could not be offered to anybody, that it did not exist for the protection of persons from arrest. It was explained that under this rule, refuge was sometimes given in times of great disorder to protect the lives of persons from immediate danger. This incident is cited merely to represent conditions which exist in Tampico, which is by far the best governed part of this Consular District.

The government is making strong efforts to open up the railroad line between Tampico and Victoria. Several days ago a construction train was sent along the line between these points. This train was accompanied by a military train carrying a force of 100 infantry and a smaller number of cavalrymen, and two field pieces. It is impossible to say when the government will succeed in opening this line. It will be even more difficult to open the telegraphic communication than the railroad as it is stated that revolutionists have torn down 100 kilometers of wires. According to the best information obtainable it appears that on May 12th (Monday), the revolutionists captured six trains between Victoria and Tampico and a number of small bridges were burned out and the revolutionists used these trains between these various points.

It was stated that when they captured the passenger train they brought the train as far as the station of Gonzalez, at which point they made all the passengers leave the train. It was said that they used the train to tear down over 100 kilometers of telegraph wires.

These alleged revolutionists between Tampico and Victoria have raided a number of American ranches and taken all the arms, ammunition, and horses that they could find. American colonists in this section are very much frightened and disturbed. Many of them have already left and many more would like to leave but are financially unable to do so.

It is stated on good authority that there are from 1000 to 1500 revolutionists surrounding Victoria, the capital of this State. It is stated that there are now 500 armed men in Victoria to defend it. It is possible that Victoria may be again attacked in the near future. All developments will be promptly reported.

Foreigners have absolutely no protection in the outlying districts in northern Tampulipas, eastern San Luis Potosi, and northern Vera Cruz. Small bands of alleged bandits raid ranches, farms, and oil camps at will. These visits are being made more frequently than in the past. The Federal military force is not strong enough to put an end to this condition. Military authorities are apparently unable to capture the persons who are guilty of robbery, assault and murder. There has been a number of such cases during the present month, some of them are as follows:

Mr. David D. Duff was assaulted with machetes by three Mexicans at Panuco, Ver. about the 1st of May. He received a number of severe cuts on the head and body but is now fully recovered. No arrests were ever made by the authorities in this case.

On May 14th Mr. James Crawford, an American boy of about 21 years of age, was stabbed in an oil camp near Panuco by a Mexican. Investigations show that the killing of Mr. Crawford was absolutely without provocation. No arrests were made in this case.

About May 1st Mr. Blagg, an American living in San Diguieto, a boy of 18 years of age, was attacked by a Mexican with a machete. Before he was able to disarm the Mexican he received a number of severe cuts. No arrests were ever made in this case.

About May 8th, Ross Carter, an American boy about 18 years old, living in San Diguieto, was attacked by a Mexican with a machete, after he had remonstrated with him for repeatedly tearing down the Carter fence in order to place cattle in the fields. Young Carter defended himself with a shot gun and slightly wounded the Mexican. Sunday, May 11th, the Mexican met A. D. Carter, brother of Ross Carter, in San Diguieto and insisted on being told the whereabouts of Ross Carter, the man who had wounded him. A. D. Carter, who is a one armed boy about 21 years old, told him several times that he did not know where his brother was. A. D. Carter went away from the Mexican but a short time later met him in a store in San Diguieto. The Mexican again molested young Carter and according to Carter's story, the Mexican put his hand to his hip as if to draw his pistol but Carter drew his own gun and shot at the Mexican, killing him instantly. He turned to leave but received a shot in the abdomen from a Mexican who was standing near by. He in turn fired at this Mexican killing him instantly. He ran but a short distance when he had to stop and was arrested. The second

Mexican who was killed proved to be one of the rurales. As he had on no uniform Carter did not know that he was an officer of the law. Carter thought that he was being fired at by one of the friends of the first Mexican. A great deal of feeling was caused by this incident and it is doubtful whether Carter will be able to secure fair trial in that district. Most of the Americans are preparing to leave because they fear further trouble. The government itself is at fault in this case because the rurales stationed there for the protection of the town consist of a band of alleged revolutionists but in reality are bandits who attempted to rob the Americans in San Diguieto some time ago.

On May 14th in Tampico, Richard Dorren, an American boy about 20 years of age, was stabbed by a Mexican. The stabbing was probably the result of a quarrel. The man who did the stabbing ran into the arms of a policeman and was immediately arrested and is still awaiting trial. The authorities granted permission for the removal of Dorren from the civil hospital to a private hospital. It is now believed that Dorren will recover.

Attempts have since been made upon lives of Mr. Crawford, father of the deceased James Crawford, and Mr. John Dye near Panuco. Indeed only a small per cent of such cases are ever reported and people realize the futility of making such reports. It is not claimed that these cases are caused by anti-American feeling but it is claimed by this office that they are due to general lawless conditions and that the cases are more numerous because of the anti-American sentiment which has been fostered by newspapers in Mexico City acting more or less with the sanction of Government officials. Authorities are powerless and are really afraid to take action in such cases.

Trains are frequently robbed. Americans as well as other passengers have to submit to having their baggage searched and their arms taken. American ranches at Isasi, Osorio and Forlon, Tamps. have been visited, their arms taken. American farmers are becoming destitute and leaving in large numbers on account of conditions. A number are now destitute in Tampico and this office is trying to arrange to send them to the United States. Practically all Americans in the colony at Las Palmas are in this class. In one American house five men rode into the kitchen on horse back and demanded arms and money. It happened in this particular case that the brother of the owner of the house was a physician and had rendered professional services to the leader. When this was found out the leader ordered his men away and gave a receipt for the gun which was taken. When Americans state that they have no arms they are not believed and are told so in so many words and are threatened. Another American colony at Colonia has become demoralized because natives in the vicinity have taken advantage of the situation and have stolen practically everything which they had. Some ranches and oil camps are visited repeatedly. Even the camps in which Americans and other foreigners have their wives are visited during the early hours of the morning and everyone must get up and allow the houses to be searched. For this reason the women have had to be brought in from the camps and sent to the United States as it is impossible to know what these bandits or alleged revolutionists will do when they become drunk.

Following extracts from letters of Mr. Burgess of Valles, S. L. P. and Dr. Tanner of Tamasopo, S. L. P. show the conditions which exist in that vicinity.

Extract of letter from Mr. Benjamin M. Burgess, C.
Valles, S. L. P.:

"Saturday morning of the 19th inst., news came of the hold-up of the train at El Abra, and immediately the Jefe Politico with the soldiers that were here, about 20, left taking the prisoners with them. They went to San Diguieto about 1:00 o'clock in the afternoon. Eight of the soldiers came back to Valles and continued guarding the place.

About 8:00 P. M. these same soldiers revolted and went to the store of the Spaniards, just across the street from my store, and demanded a large amount of money. On being refused they began shooting at any one in sight, about 100 shots were fired but no one killed that I know of. The soldiers during the shooting managed to rob the safe of about $600.00 of the money belonging to the Spaniards. The soldiers then left and robbed people that they met on the road as they went.

Monday morning reports circulated that the rebel force from El Abra was nearing the town which proved true, and about noon they arrived at the outskirts of the town and demanded the place, by the leader Manuel Larraga, at the head of about 50 men. The rebels agreed not to sack the town if they were given 1000 pesos and agreed to leave as soon as the money was raised which occupied about four hours. The merchants raised the money and the rebels left. As before, I had to contribute to this fund. There is very little safety here now but most of the American families like myself cannot get out as all that we have is invested here.

I have just received notice from the Department of Reclamaciones, refusing to pay the claim, alleging that the signatures are of persons not recognized as leaders of the revolution. My claim was one of many of a like nature and I suppose all will be refused. I would be greatly obliged to you if you could get from our Ambassador in Mexico, the receipts which you sent to him, as I should like to use them, I am going to prove my good faith in the matter at any rate."

Extract of letter from Dr. H. B. Tanner,
Tamasopo, S. L. P.:

"Last Friday night (the 9th) a freight train that was coming this
way was exploded, the locomotive boiler, at Tambaco, about 10
kilometers from here. It seems the train was passing Tambaco at a great
speed and the conductor sent the brakeman ahead to see what was the
matter. He found both the engineer and fireman asleep, (been on duty
22 hours). He halloed to them and as the fireman awoke he saw no
water in the water gauges and started to inject cold water. The
brakeman got scared and ran as fast as he could back, when he
reached the fifth car from the engine, the boiler exploded, killing the
engineer and fireman as well as one of our men from here who was
riding next to the engine on the top of a freight car.

Saturday the passenger train coming this way from Tampico was
held up by a band of rebels at El Abra. The number was variously
stated as from 75 to 300, I guess the former was nearer correct. They
robbed the passengers of all valuables as well as broke open baggage
and express and appropriated anything of value they could find; the
passengers were not injured. Later the train was permitted to proceed.
The authorities, not being able to get the operator at El Abra and
suspecting trouble, did not permit the passenger train to pass
Cardenas, the one that was coming from San Luis Potosi, but turned it
back from there. The rebels at El Abra attempted to destroy the bridge
at Choy but did not succeed in doing any damage to speak of.

No trains were run from this time till Thursday following. On
Sunday a freight train left Tamasopo station for Cardenas and at Las
Canoas the engineer uncoupled to water, and all, and the hand brakes
not being set the train started back and wrecked itself in tunnel
number 2. Eight cars were demolished and much merchandise destroyed,
including two very large fine dynamos for the Puebla tram line.

On Tuesday a band of rebels came via Tambaco to Tamasopo,
numbering about 60. They burned the houses of the Chinamen in

Tamasopo, smashed the instruments in the Railway Station and tore up the papers and books. Looted the store at Tamasopo, kept infanta. All got drunk and yelled "Death to the Americans". They sent two messengers to our office at Agua Buena, saying they were coming over here peaceably if they could but if not, by force. We sent word back that if the leader wished to come he was welcome but we would not permit any number of armed men to come over. About this time, 4:00 P.M., a military train was seen on the mountain and the rebels mounted their horses and skedaddled to the hills.

125 soldiers detrained at Tamasopo and came over to Agua Buena for the night, we felt considerably relieved to have them here, but rather worried to have them go the next day to Valles, altho the Colonel promised to be back here today for our pay day.

Passing pens tell us of the presence of a number of bands of bandits in the mountains all about here and yesterday we learnt Ciudad del Maiz was attacked and taken as the soldiers there, some 25 left the day before for Alaquaines and most of the inhabitants of both places left for Cardenas and on to San Luis Potosi.

If we are left in reasonable peace we will finish our crop in three weeks and then we will get out of the country if we can.

Probably the presence of troops passing up and down the line will prevent any destruction to the Railway property and they will be able to operate trains, at least this is reasonable until such time as the rebels gather enough men with arms and ammunition to think they are strong enough to cope with what few troops there are in this neighborhood.

It is a common remark among our men here that as soon as we close down and there is no more work that there is nothing for them to do but to join the rebels. I understand that Rascon has closed down and so more than likely before long there will be plenty of rebels in this region who being out of work and can muster any kind of an old arm will intimidate any one who has anything they want. As they get used to the game and see how easy it is to live without work they probably will get blood-thirsty like they have in Morelos and then it is kill as well as rob.

Anyway, I hope we can get away before their education is much further advanced."

The following extracts from letters received from Dr. W. J. Hancock and Mr. H. T. McCabe show the conditions which exist in the vicinity of San Diguieto, S. L. P.

****

Extract from letter received from Dr. W. J. Hancock:

"About 50 or more soldiers arrived here two days since. The eighteen or twenty that were here already stay here at all times now. The extra 50 are supposed to go out after the rebels that come to this vicinity.

The 40 rurales that came here Saturday night with the Jefe from Valles have the same leaders that the band had that came through here some weeks ago and robbed the town. You have heard of the trouble here of last Sunday, one American killing two Mexicans, which happened in the morning. I was sent for by the Jefe Politico in about an hour after the shooting and he said the feeling against the Americans was high. That the people wanted to kill Carter but he had ordered all Mexicans to bring their arms to him and that he wanted to protect the Americans if I would personally guarantee that they would stay at home on that day and arouse no further trouble. I told him that I would guarantee the same personally if he would do the same for his people, which he agreed to do and seemed quite reasonable but later got very indignant at me when I protested against them moving Carter too soon. Accused me of sending the messages and said he was not taking orders from the U. S. but left Carter here until yesterday. Mr. Blagg called here at my house Sunday evening at four o'clock and said that the man's brother that was killed had been to Mr. Carter's three times that day, cursing the old folks, or parents, of the boy who did the shooting, and threatening to kill them. He went on the porch once with a knife. Mr. Blagg said he had reported him to the Jefe but nothing had been done. I went with him, to the Jefe and he told me that the man was then under arrest. I learned the next morning that he was not arrested at all. But he has given no more trouble but has not been seen here any more.

Now I would like to have your advice. The Americans are doing their part, staying away from them and having no more trouble or giving offense any way. Would like to know what you think about us staying here. Most of us have all we have invested here and could take nothing with us if we leave here. There are some who would not have money enough to get out and there are none that would have anything left. What is your opinion about sending the women and children out.

The rebels seem to be getting worse."

Extract from letter received from Mr. H. T.
McCabe:

May 17. Day before yesterday 75 Federal cavalry arrived here (San
Diguieto) from San Luis Potosi and Pedro Rodriguez with his Valles
bunch are the same who levied on this town and on Valles some time
ago and the soldier or rurale (bandit) that Carter killed was one of his
crowd. This A.M. a special train with a heavy guard transferred Carter
to Valles so he is now under the charitable and philanthropic protection
of the gang, one of whom he killed and they will no doubt be
exceedingly pleasant with him the dead rurale was also a resident of
Valles. The order for Carter's removal, so I am informed, was made by
the Jefe Politico of Valles, and he dare make no order except as he may
be instructed by Pedro Rodriguez, the Captain of the gang. Rodriguez
and his gang were here having brought the prisoners from Valles as
they were expecting an attack on Valles by the revolutionists who swore
they would execute the Jefe Politico, so the Jefe fled with the
Rodriguez gang and was domiciled here. The Federals who came in here
Thursday from San Luis Potosi had orders to shoot the Jefe Politico so
he was between both fires but it seems that Rodriguez intervened and
saved him for the time being. Therefore the Jefe Politico owes his life
to Rodriguez and it is only natural to suppose that the Jefe makes his
orders only on the approval or command of Rodriguez.

I have the inside Mexican version of the Carter affair and can
assure you CONFIDENTIALLY, for thus I received my information, that
Carter has not the remotest chance of ever gaining his liberty and I
would not give much for his life among the gang over at Valles. The
Mexican feeling against Carter is intensely bitter which included
Rodriguez and the Jefe Politico.

In addition to the foregoing I have just learned that M. I. Vought,
an American living at Xicotencatl, was seriously wounded while
attempting to protect his wife and her sister from attacks from two
drunken members of the 21st. Reg. Revolutionists. Castro, the leader,
punished the two men but the incident indicates that American women

are not safe in these outlying districts. I have talked to Col. Betancourt, the new Military Commander at Tampico and he has advised me to ask the women to be brought in. He also suggested that all Americans be brought in to Tampico from outlying districts but later stated that he would wire the Government asking if a force could not be sent to the Chamal district to afford proper protection. He is expecting about 1000 men which are to be used in Southern Tamaulipas and it is a part of this force which he wishes to send to the Chamal and Xicotencatl district. If he does not get a favorable reply, I will notify all American farmers to come into Tampico as Col. Betancourt is not in a position to afford protection otherwise.

I have just been informed that a band of 11 alleged revolutionists entered the house of the Buckley family at El Chote. These men were well armed and were not content with taking all of the arms and horses but demanded money. The Buckleys who are really poor people denied having any money and the bandits brought out a rope and prepared a noose and threatened to hang the men - at least that is what the men understood from the motions which they were making. The Buckleys then weakened and gave them 100 pesos which was all of the money which they had in the house.

The Buckleys consist of three families or 14 persons all of whom are now destitute in this city and asking transportation to the U. S. There are now 60 persons from the outlying districts in the city desiring such transportation because they are destitute and cannot continue on their farms having lost their crops, time, money, etc. If transportation can be furnished this number will probably be increased to 200.

As a result of these conditions this office sent a cipher telegram recommending that the Captain of the U.S.S. Connecticut be instructed to take action. The matter has undoubtedly been brought to the attention of the Federal Government as additional troops are now on the way, according to information received from the American Ambassador.

Col. Rivera, who has been Jefe de las Armas in Tampico during the last few weeks has been promoted to be Jefe de las Armas in Victoria and Col. Betancourt, who had charge of the defense of Victoria when it was attacked some weeks ago has arrived and has taken charge of this post. This change is undoubtedly due to complaints by Mexicans that they had no guarantees because of a number of arrests on charge of conspiracy against the Government. Col. Betancourt stated to me, that notwithstanding the fact that the U. S. had not recognized Mexico, he had received specific instructions from the Minister of War to afford proper protection to the Americans and their interests.

There was a determined effort made by the friends of Col. Rivera to have him retained at Tampico. People thought that because of his youth and inexperience he greatly exaggerated conditions in Tampico. Others think that the associates whom he had here were interested in securing gambling concessions and also in selling horses, supplies, etc. for the force of 100 men for which the alleged voluntary contributions were secured. To say the least there has been no excuse for the alarming accounts which have been given out regarding the Tampico situation as it has never been in the slightest danger.

The new Military Commander is said to be thoroughly acquainted with conditions and people in this part of the State and his appointment is said to be entirely satisfactory to those who have opposed Col. Rivera. It is said that he has a great many enemies and that he is unusually severe as he is supposed to have been responsible for the severe measures taken in Victoria after the attack which was made upon it some time ago.

The great difficulty is that this district lies partly in three states and the Tampico officials have jurisdiction over only a small part of it. The Tampico Military Commander now has jurisdiction over a part of

Tamaulipas just out of Tampico. The Victoria Military Commander has jurisdiction over the central part of the State. The Military Commander at San Luis Potosi and the Military Commander at Vera Cruz respectively have jurisdiction over the parts of those states which are in this district. These latter districts are adjacent to Tampico while the Military Commanders are so far away that they have no adequate idea of conditions. Public reports have greatly exaggerated conditions in Tampico but have ignored conditions in the outlying districts where they have been the most deplorable.

Attached hereto are clippings from the Tampico Times and the Republica. These clippings bear on a movement that was fostered by the Jefe de las Armas, Col. Rivera, for the arrest of Mr. Frank Hamrick, an American citizen, who is editor on the Tampico Times on the charge of mixing in Mexican Politics. The article was unwise under existing conditions but really consisted of clippings from old Mexican newspapers. I took Mr. Hamrick before the Military Commander and had him state that in publishing the article he had had no bad intentions toward the Government. I also had him furnish a proper translation of same. I also saw the publishers of La Republica and suggested that the notoriety which was being given to the matter was unwise as it only created anti-American feeling. The latter ceased publishing articles in regard to the matter and the Government has as yet not arrested Mr. Hamrick although the matter was consigned to the Federal Court on May 24th.

Every effort is being made to avoid discussions or actions which might give rise to ill feeling between Mexicans and foreigners. The authorities suppressed the publication of a local sheet, the El Gallitto, which published an aritcle which was intended to inflame Mexicans against the U. S. I merely called attention to the article without requesting action.

Mexican newspapers (Mexico City) contained articles which had a bad effect but these also seem to have been discontinued.

The American Colony of this Consular District are organizing an association for social and benevolent purposes. The organization will be perfected on June 2nd, in this city.

I have the honor to be, Sir,

Your obedient servant,
(signed) Clarence Arkell
American Consul.

Dept. State 4 copies.
Embassy - copy.
Consul General Monterey - copy.
Rear Admiral Beatty - copy.
Capt. Knapp - U.S.S. Connecticut - copy.

Law Offices
HAFF, MESERVEY, GERMAN & MICHAELS
Suite 606 Commerce Building
KANSAS CITY, MO.

Mexico City, D. F.,
May 28th, 1913.

The President,
White House,
Washington, D. C.

Distinguished Sir:

Complying with my promise made to you in personal conversation before I left Washington for Mexico, to write you my observation of conditions here after my arrival and investigation, I have the honor to submit the following brief relation of facts, time not permitting more, as the mail for the Ward Line boat will close at two o'clock today, and there will be no other mail for the United States until one week later.

I arrived in Mexico City Friday morning last, this being the sixth day since my arrival, but my extensive acquaintance has enabled me to make good progress in familiarizing myself with the actual conditions. I have carefully read all the daily papers, both Spanish and English, and conversed with all classes in order to thoroughly sound public sentiment. I have daily conferences with Senator Manuel Calero, formerly Minister of Foreign Affairs in President Madero's Cabinet and Ambassador of Mexico to the United States, who is my most intimate friend of many years standing. Yesterday, I had an interview of nearly two hours with the Minister of Education of President Huerta's Cabinet, also an intimate friend, who gave me a full and reliable history of political events since my last visit here. I also had lunch with General Garcia Cuellar, Governor of the Federal District, at which were present among others, Mr. De Lima, Manager of the Bank of Commerce and

Industry - the representative here of Messrs. Speyer & Company, bankers, of New York and London; Mr. Beck, President of Mexico City Banking Company; Mr. Whiffin, representative of the Associated Press; Mr. Murray, correspondent of the New York Tribune and World; Dr. Hale, correspondent of "The Worlds Work"; Hon. Arnold Shanklin, Consul General of the United States; and Licenciado Manuel Calero, member of the Mexican Senate. From these various advantageous sources, I have gained a pretty good idea of present conditions here, political and commercial.

Immediately upon arrival, I explained to the fullest extent of my ability to Senator Calero, the state of public sentiment in the United States and especially upon the very important and debated question of recognition of the Huerta Government by the United States. I explained to Senator Calero that in what I stated, I must not be understood as having the knowledge or the authority to express the views of the Washington Administration; but that, in my opinion, a pre-requisite of the recognition desired would be to convince the Washington Government of the intention of the Huerta Administration to cause a national election to be held in the Mexican Republic at a reasonably early date, at which the Mexican people would have the opportunity, without intimidation or interference, to express their choice for a President to be elected according to law and duly inaugurated as constitutional-successor of the present interim Administration. Senator Calero stated to me that he was sure that this was the desire and honest intention of President Huerta, that the form of holding election had been recently changed by constitutional amendment, that there was not as yet election law passed by Congress under which an election could be held, although the President had set the date of October 26th next, but that certain factions in Congress were opposing the election law for various reasons, some believing that an election should not be called until the beginning of next year after the country was thoroughly pacified, others because they hope to make political capital against the Huerta Administration by postponing the election, thus giving the revolutionary factions the opportunity to say that the President has no <u>bona fide</u> intention of permitting an election to be held.

My statement confirmed Senator Calero in his own opinion, of the importance of the passage of the election law before the adjournment of Congress, and he proceeded with three other Senators immediately to interview the President, who not only was heartily in accord with this policy, but asked their honest assistance in pushing the bill through in Congress. Senator Calero and the Committee spent all of Sunday in perfecting the form of the bill and on Monday morning it was a special order of the House of Deputies and is now pending with the best prospects of passage, as the President is evidently using all of his influence in its favor, in good faith. I say good faith for the simple reason that everyone of the Administration newspapers are strongly urging the passage of the bill, and this would not be if the President did not earnestly desire it.

A member of the President's Cabinet, an intimate friend of mine, assured me that the election would be fairly conducted with every guaranty; that it has been made a matter of Cabinet discussion, that he made the statement that he would not remain in the Cabinet except this could be assured, and the President had warmly approved his determination, and he was absolutely sure of the President's good faith. The President stated that he has made this promise to the Nation and he proposes to fulfill it.

I think, therefore, that before the adjournment of Congress, the election will be definitely assured by law to take place on October 26th, which, under present conditions, I have been convinced is as early as it could be held giving reasonable opportunity for the pacification of the country and for the necessary political discussion and enlightenment of voters. It is certain that there will be two or more candidates and that General Felix Diaz will be hotly opposed by the liberal candidates.

The second matter of importance is that the Government has succeeded in placing a loan with French and English bankers aided by Speyer & Company of New York and some other American bankers in the sum of two hundred million pesos. This loan has already been approved by Congress and the first installment of twenty million dollars was delivered to the Government yesterday. This loan was supported also by the formal recognition of the Huerta Administration by the Governments of Great Britain, France and, I am informed, by all other European nations, with the single exception of Russia.

The plan of the Government is to increase the army to eighty thousand men and for that purpose Congress has appropriated thirty million pesos for immediate use.

The result of this general recognition of the Huerta Government and the successful placing of the loan has been greatly to strengthen confidence and has produced a cheerful and optimistic feeling here. Exchange immediately fell to 2.05, whereas it was formerly as high as 2.40 and could not be obtained at that price.

FORECAST OF CONDITIONS

It is, of course, a matter of some peril always to attempt to forecast political conditions, especially under circumstances as difficult as those that surround the situation here. Nevertheless, I think the fact that I repeatedly visited this city and various other parts of the Republic during the past year, not only at the beginning of the Madero Administration, and spent six weeks here at the time of the inauguration of the Revolution in the North by Pascual Orozco, and had during that time intimate connection with political affairs and association with members of Madero's Cabinet, and was also here in December last, at the close of the Madero regime, and carefully noted the conditions of public sentiment and the trend of political affairs, now enables me better to appreciate present conditions than if I have no knowledge extending back of the present time.

I note the following difference between the two periods: last year, when the Revolution of the North under General Orozco began against Madero, he did not have the cordial and frank support of certain capitalistic or mercantile classes of the country, nor did he have the support of any of the political parties or divisions, with the single exception of what was known as the "Porra", which consisted largely of a selfish, ambitious class of politicians, who had no other interest in the success of the Madero Administration than in bringing ahead their own selfish and ambitious plans for personal and political aggrandizement. All efforts to bring to the support of the Government the most influential elements of society here, were without success; but when I visited the city last December conditions had actually grown worse, though they were apparently improved in some other parts of the Republic.

I also noted another feeling with regard to the Madero Government, which was a certain lack of confidence in its success and in its sanity and serious purposes. It seemed to be a prevalent opinion that Madero was a dreamer, without the practical ability to solve the problems with which he was confronted and the difficulties which he had raised by the Revolution that he fomented.

At the present time I note a different state of public opinion. The most influencial classes here, both political and social, as well as business, are united in the support of the Huerta Administration, and are lending their aid to the Government for the pacification of the country, with the single exception of the radical Maderistas, who, under the Madero Administration, formed the body of the so-called "Porra", but these are in the minority in the Chamber of Deputies, and when you come to consider the society at large, the business and social classes that are worth considering, the "Porra" element forms but a small minority. In other words, the general feeling here at the present time seems to be that the Huerta Administration is a serious Administration honestly engaged in the pacification of the country, and with the intention of fulfilling its promises to re-establish order and peace, and to bring about the election of a President to succeed Huerta by constitutional means. The press of the city is almost unanimous in favor of the Administration here, as the press under the Madero regime was largely against it. When you add to this fact the business element throughout the Republic, not only here but in the States where the insurgents are in control, is, of course, exceedingly anxious for peace, it seems to me that we have forces to work that promise much for ultimate success.

When you consider the lethargic character of the so-called "peon" class, and the unimportant figure which they cut in the matter of shaping the destinies of the country at the present time, and when you consider the further fact that the revolutionists in the North are practically without funds and seem to have exhausted their sources of obtaining them, and with great difficulty will be able to obtain arms and ammunition, I cannot see how we can expect them to succeed, and it seems to me that the Federal Government from all points of view must reasonably be expected to succeed, unless some change in sentiment - which cannot now be predicted - should occur. This being the case, it seems to me that within the next three months, unless the revolutionists lay down their arms and make some compromise with the present Federal Government and join hands with them in supporting law and order, and bringing about a constitutional election, the Federal Government will succeed in any event, and the revolutionists will be defeated and suppressed.

I find that the papers of the North and the revolutionists of the North, have not correctly represented the character of the present Huerta Administration. It does not appear to be that severe, tyrannical government which has been described in the press of the North, but I find similar liberty of speech and of the press here as existed under Madero. The House of Deputies is entirely independent, noisy and unruly, and seems to have no fear whatever of the Administration. I never saw the time in Mexico when the Mexican Congress appeared so independent and fearless as it is at the present time. These facts deprive the Revolutionists of many of the grounds which they put forward as justification for their open rebellion. My observation shows that the revolutionists of the North do not understand the Mexicans of the center, and vice-versa, the Mexicans of the center do not understand the purposes and aims of the revolutionists of the North. I sincerely hope that they may get together without much more bloodshed and destruction of property and credit.

This letter is dictated to my private Secretary to assure its confidential character; and is mailed in a sealed envelope to Mr. Cleveland H. Dodge, New York, with request that he re-mail the same to you.

Without more, I have the honor to subscribe myself,

Your obedient servant,
(signed) Delbert J. Haff

DJH/s

CURTIS, MALLET-PREVOST & COLT,
Attorneys and Counsellors at Law
30 Broad Street, New York.

PERSONAL   June 5, 1913.

To the Honorable William Jennings Bryan,
     Secretary of State,
          Washington, D. C.

Dear Mr. Secretary:

In accordance with the offer which I made yesterday and which you kindly accepted, I enclose herewith copy of the letter which I am today writing to the President with reference to the Mexican situation.

     Believe me,

                              Very sincerely yours,

                                   (signed) S. Mallet-Prevost

SMP/s

(Encl.)

CURTIS, MALLET-PREVOST & COLT
Attorneys and Counsellors at Law
30 Broad Street, New York

June 5, 1913.

To the Honorable Woodrow Wilson,
    President of the United States,
        Washington, D. C.

Dear Mr. President:

In a letter dated May 21st Mr. Tumulty informed me that he had brought to your attention a letter from Secretary Garrison stating that I had recently been to Mexico and that you might wish to hear my views with regard to the political situation in that country. Mr. Tumulty further informed me that you would be pleased to receive my observations in writing. In compliance with that request, I have the honor of addressing you.

Permit me by way of introduction to make a brief statement with reference to myself.

I have all my life had intimate social and business relations with Mexicans. In years gone by I have at times acted as counsel for the Mexican government. During the past thirty years I have visited the country frequently. In connection with the special work to which I have devoted my professional life I have endeavored to familiarize myself and keep myself in touch with conditions in Spanish-America, and especially in Mexico. I have had the honor of serving our own Government as special counsel in various international questions having to do with Latin America, the first time during the administration of President Cleveland. I have for the past five years represented an important American and British claim against Mexico, which claim has recently been settled. In connection with this special matter I was in Mexico City all of last April and part of May, and during that period I had the opportunity of personally acquainting myself with the situation. I spoke with most of the men who are today politically prominent, and with many who were former supporters of Madero. I have at present no questions of any kind pending in Mexico, and no personal interest in favor of or against the present government. My only financial interests in the country consist of shares in a concern which has not greatly suffered by the revolutions of the past three years and which, so far as I can see, is not likely to be affected by a change of government. I think, therefore, that I can fairly describe myself as an unbiased observer. My motives in addressing you are that, as an American citizen, and as one interested in Mexico, I wish to contribute my mite towards cementing the friendly relations between the two countries; and that, as a life-long Democrat, I should like to assist your administration if I can, by furnishing you with such information as I have.

With apologies for these personal references I beg to submit the following for your consideration:

The movement which resulted in the overthrow of the Madero government was inspired and carried out by General Felix Diaz, General Mondragon and their immediate followers. Although those who fought were a mere handful, they nevertheless voiced the profound dissatisfaction of the Mexican people at large with an administration that was regarded as a failure. To the average thinking Mexican, Madero, at first an idealist and reformer, had, under the influence of unprincipled councillors and of a corrupt family, become a tyrant. Those who had at first believed in his promises and who had relied upon his ability and determination to carry them out, were disappointed to find that the old abuses continued and even multiplied, and that the only effect of the revolution had apparently been to make matters worse. So firmly, however, were the Maderos intrenched in power, and so lavish in dispensing the nation's money among their friends and supporters, that it required unusual courage to attempt their overthrow. The attempt was nevertheless made, and had been carried to a successful issue, before General Huerta offered to ally himself with the triumphant party. A rejection of his offer could hardly have had any effect upon the ultimate result--no longer in doubt--but it would certainly have entailed further bloodshed; wishing to avoid this, Generals Diaz and Mondragon accepted the terms proposed by General Huerta, and it was agreed that he should become Provisional President.

I lay stress upon these facts because it seems to me important to distinguish between the personality of General Huerta and the movement of which he, at the last moment, became a part. During the inception and development of that movement General Huerta had no share in it--on the contrary, he was the champion of Madero and the most prominent exponent of the system which had made it possible for the Madero government to continue in power; his final defection was an eloquent proof of his own defeat; and his subsequent identification with the victorious rebels can hardly avail to disguise his true character or to deceive anyone respecting the relation which he bore toward the revolution. Of course, General Huerta as Provisional President of Mexico is, under the laws of that country, the Executive, vested with all the powers that appertain to his office and so identified with the national entity as to make it difficult to distinguish between his personality and the government of which he forms an essential part; and yet if the question of recognition, which affects the whole nation, is to hinge upon the morality of General Huerta's conduct, it seems not improper to consider how far the nation at large can fairly be made to suffer the consequences of his alleged misdeeds.

In line with what I have already said, let me mention two further facts:

First. The agreement which terminated the fighting between the Diaz-Mondragon and the Madero forces last February, while it raised General Huerta to the Presidency, provided him with a cabinet which was not of his choosing; it was what might fairly be called a coalition cabinet, representing the Diaz-Mondragon combination, the Orozco revolution, the Reyes party, and in general all the elements that had been actively or passively opposed to Madero. It is probably not too much to say that if General Huerta had been free to select his own cabinet, not one of the ministers whom he has would today be at his council table.

Second. If General Huerta were quite free to act according to his own will, it is the general belief that the election of his successor would be indefinitely postponed. The fact that he is not wholly free was evidenced in April last by his inability to resist the pressure placed upon him by his cabinet when, after the defeat of the election bill in Congress, all the ministers, with one exception, tendered their resignations. General Huerta was unwilling to face the situations which would have been created had he accepted those resignations, and he therefore chose the only remaining alternative, and consented to the holding of the election, on October 26th next.

I mention these two incidents to show that, in a very real sense, the government of Mexico at this time is a cabinet government rather than a presidential government; and that the cabinet, and therefore the government, represents elements with which General Huerta personally has little to do. In one respect--and one only, so far as I am informed--has any important thing been done without the co-operation of the cabinet. I refer to the killing of the ex-President and Vice-President. How far, if at all, General Huerta may have been implicated in that killing, I am not prepared to say; but even assuming his complicity, I have no hesitation in saying that not a single one of his ministers had any part in, or even knew of, the plot until it was actually carried out. While all the ministers believe that an impartial investigation into the conduct of Madero and Suarez would have resulted in conviction and execution, they deprecate the barbarity with which justice was in fact meted out. Of course, if the cabinet believed that General Huerta was privy to the killing, they might have resigned as a protest against the act; but it is at least questionable whether, at that crisis, before the provisional government was well in the saddle, and while the political situation was still trembling in the balance, the cabinet would have been justified in abandoning the only government that for the moment existed, thereby possibly plunging the country again into bloodshed. For that one act, attributed to General Huerta, the Mexican people have already been made to pay dearly, and the question which I venture to submit is whether the demands of justice and morality require that the nation should continue still further to suffer?

I say that the Mexican people have already paid dearly, because the withholding of recognition has to a great extent tied the hands of the government and made it well nigh impossible to take effective measures toward the suppression of the murder and rapine that are devastating the land. Our attitude has contributed not a little to encourage revolution, to fan the ambitions of unprincipled adventurers, and to keep alive movements that, having neither inherent merit nor elements of success, would have collapsed long since but for the belief that the United States desires the downfall of the Huerta government. The belief, on the other hand, is general among thinking Mexicans that the present government is Mexico's last hope; through the cabinet, that government represents the best elements in the country; it is making a sincere effort to re-establish order and morality in the finances and in the army; it commands the best military and civil talent; and it is impossible to believe that if it should fall any other combination could be found so well qualified to deal with the situation. Mexico has had two successful revolutions in less than three years. Every new successful revolt must bring with it a fresh crop of aspirants for presidential honors; and the disorders and anarchy which now prevail in many sections of the country must spread, thus bringing the country nearer and nearer to the verge of foreign intervention.

When Secretary Garrison gave me his letter of introduction, and when I had hoped for the honor of a personal interview with you, it had been my intention to urge other reasons in favor of recognition--reasons which have to do wholly with American interests and American policy. In the meantime, however, I have been fortunate enough to lay my views before the Secretary of State, and I learned from him that the main obstacle in the way of recognition lay in the disinclination of the United States Government to recognize a man who is believed to be responsible for the killing of Madero and Suarez. In writing today, therefore, I have addressed myself exclusively to that point, and have endeavored to distinguish between the man Huerta and the government and nation which for the moment he happens to represent. If you desire information from me upon any other phase of the situation it will give me great pleasure to respond.

    I have the honor to be,

                                    Very respectfully yours,
                                    (signed) S. Mallet-Prevost

SMP/s

THE REVOLUTION IN SOMBRERETE, ZACATECAS

Chalchihuites
June 8th, 1913.

Dear Sir:

I have no letter of yours to acknowledge for we are without any mail here, none having gone in or out of Sombrerete since a week ago yesterday. All my previous letters to you are, I suppose, held up there, so will try and give you in this letter an idea of the happenings in this district during the past week, as this letter will be taken by one of our couriers to Zacatecas. This man will leave Dulces Nombres tomorrow very early and should reach you some time next Thursday.

Conditions during the past week have gone from bad to worse, and all this district is very badly in need of some help and federal soldiers. I now regret having to report the complete sacking of Sombrerete, not only of all the stores and pawn-shops, but also of a number of private houses. Ever since last Monday rebels have been in possession of Sombrerete. The Jefe Politico there, I suppose believing that help was coming from them in view of the Governors telegram of the 31st May saying that the troops which had routed the rebels at Fresnillo were coming on to Sombrerete, with the eight or ten men he has, repulsed one or two of the small bands that tried to enter the town, but every day these kept increasing in number, until the defenders had to leave the town at the mercy of these devils. Two or three private citizens, among them one Spaniard, Carlos Corrales, were killed. Three or four of the rebels were also killed among these being Tirso Contreras, the leader of the band that came here two weeks ago yesterday and who afterwards visited La Noria. The fact that this man was killed was more than sufficient cause for these devils to commit their usual acts of depredations, and the men who had come from Sombrerete, say the place is sad to look upon, as there isn't a single store that has anything in it except the shelving and counters, that several of the private houses are wide open everything they had having been taken out, that no one of the middle or better class people can be seen on the streets, that these are lined with empty packing cases, and in fact that there is complete desolation there. A band of these men have been at "Los Tocayos" all these days trying to find Mr. Heldt, and according to reports they wanted to blow up the mines, buildings, etc. but were prevented from doing this by the workmen and their women who said that if these properties were destroyed their only means of livelihood would be taken away from them, and at last succeeded in saving them. Mr. Heldt is believed to be hiding in one of the mines, and up to date has not been found. From Mr. Naude I have absolutely no news, but believe he is safe, as when I was last in Sombrerete he told me he had a fine hiding place where he would never be found, he did not tell me where this place was however. I have written to him twice during the week, but of course have received no reply. All this information has been gathered by us here from men who come from there but as some of these are trustworthy men, there is no doubt in our mind but what it must all be true, especially as all reports agree. From all this you will gather that Sombrerete has suffered more during the past week, than any town in the State of Zacatecas since the revolution of 1910, and unless they can get some help there, and soon, there is absolutely no reason why these devils should not continue their work of destruction and Sombrerete will not be the only town that will be practically wiped out. Chalchihuites may come next, though I doubt if any large band will come here, as they know the pitiful condition of the place, and that they could not get food here for more than one day. Ever since railway communication with Durango was cut off, Chalchihuites has been supplying itself from Sombrerete, but now of course this is out of the question, and by tomorrow or the day after we will be entirely out of some of the staple goods such as sugar, coffee, etc.

I had got this far in the letter when Jose Dolores Castaneda (the telegraph operator and Admor. del Timbre of this town) came in here to see me. He left with me for Sombrerete last week, has been there ever since, and returned here late last night. He brought me a message from Mr. Naude whom he saw last yesterday morning, to the effect that he was safe and up to that time nothing had been done to the agency. It seems that Mr. Naude, Castaneda and several others were hiding in one of the convents and that they have had a very hard time indeed. Mr. Naude sent word that the situation was unbearable, and that he is going to get out the first opportunity that presents itself, as he cannot stand it any longer. He mentioned to Castaneda my going there to see him and talk this over, and I will do so as soon as I know that the coast is clear. If only a garrison could be sent out there, it would make this people feel much better and bring them a little peace of mind. Castaneda informs me that while not every store was sacked, there are only one or two that escaped, and that the rest of the rumors received here were true. When he left there yesterday noon, the rebels were still in town sacking what they could find, but that most of them had left saying they were on their way to Durango. He also informs me that Jesus Morillo, the Jefe Politico, left Tuesday for Zacatecas to place the situation before the Government and to get some help if he possibly could, so the chances are that by this time you know all about this news but perhaps not with all the details herein given.

Part of the men who were at Sombrerete went to La Noria last Tuesday and Mr. Coxe had to give up three hundred pesos as per his enclosed note. I am writing to him that I may manage to get him about one thousand cupels for next week.

In this immediate vicinity, we have had small bands prowling around all week, and while they have not tried to enter town there is nothing to prevent their so doing. In all the nearby ranches they have been committing their usual acts, taking away the corn beans and every other eatable they could find, killing cattle, taking horses, breaking furniture and at two of the ranches they have carried off girls. One of these was fourteen years old, and the other was about 18 and she was carried away on her wedding day. There is absolutely nothing around here to prevent these men doing just as they please, and while I realize that it is hard for the Government to send garrisons to every place, still it would require but few men to clean this district out, as most of the bands that are around here are very poorly armed and are short of ammunition. In Chalchihuites, the same as Sombrerete there are no longer any authorities, for while the parties are here, they pay absolutely no attention to their offices. Very few, if any, of the men around here are paying their taxes, and the result is that the Recaudacion has no funds and the Government employees, including the young lady school teachers, have not been paid for several decenas, and they are now reaching the point where they have no more money with which to buy their food, and as you may imagine the prices of some of the staple articles have now reached figures almost prohibitive for the poor people. The situation in all is far worse than it ever has been before, and worse even perhaps than the Government realizes, and unless we get help of some kind soon it is not hard to forecast what the sad end will be. I hate writing such bad reports from here, for I realize perfectly that you are doing everything you can to help us out, but it is well for you to know exactly how we stand, and that this cannot keep up much longer, for if it does, the men will either have to join the rebels, or start robbing and looting on their own account in order to get food.

Last night I received a letter from Mr. Arkell dated the 5th and am enclosing one for you from him. In his letter to me he states that they are going to repair this line again and that trains left Durango on the 5th for Rio Chico to get ties for this purpose, and also that Mr. Tabler was going to Canitas to start the work on all the camps between there and Sombrerete as the Government has decided to do this in order to give work to all the men who are now without it. I hope all this is true, but as he says, we cannot believe it until the work is actually started. He without doubt gives you the same news. He tells me in his letter that he is enclosing a check to you for expenses of telegrams etc. sent by last messenger. As that office has already charged this one with that amount, and I have credited same, I will thank you to give the necessary instructions to have the amount of Mr. Arkell's check credited to this office in order to balance this account.

A report has just reached us (11:30 A.M.) that a band of rebels is coming this way from Laborcita, about 8 kilometers from here, but as we get so many of these, shall try and get the mail off with the courier at all events. All the stores are being closed right now, and the usual panic has started among the people.

At Canutillo we have not been molested now for several days. Last Monday four men went there and got $4.39 from the Station agent, but did not even go to our little office there. We now have three watchmen down there, one during the day and two at night. Last week while they were bringing down the last lot from Dulces Nombres, some seven sacks of ore were stolen by the arrieron, and though we have found out where this ore is, and asked the authorities to make a cateo of the house, and recuperate this ore, they told us in the first place that the ranch where it is pertains to the Sombrerete district, and in the second that even though it were in this district, that they could do nothing as no one would go to make this cateo. With Sombrerete in the condition it is at present, it is even useless to go try and get anything done, so here is a case of absolute robbery, where the goods are found, and one is helpless and cannot recover them.

As stated above, I shall go to Sombrerete the very first opportunity that presents itself and have a talk with Mr. Naude and should he decide to leave, I will as per your previous instructions receive everything there, and shall expect you, when you reply to this, to give me some further instructions or to state whether or not the previous ones stand. I don't suppose there will be for some time to come, but the place could be kept going even though only on small scale.

I will appreciate it very much if you will kindly have one hundred dollars gold to Mrs. Turnbull, c/o Dr. G. Graham Watts, 102 Ninth St.

or Post Office Box No. 745, San Antonio. I have the money here to pay for this, I will credit same to that office as soon as I receive the Nota de Cargo. You will be the best judge as to how to send this money, either by mail in a draft, Postal Order, or Telegraph order. Whichever is the safest and quickest way for it to get there.

I don't suppose that the rebels in Sombrerete will stay there indefinitely, and perhaps during the coming week we may again have mail service through there. I shall at all times try and keep you posted of conditions around this district and hope in a short time I may be able to make a more favorable report. I shall of course stay here and look after your interests to the best of my ability, and hope that your answer to this letter will bring some encouraging news.

[Unsigned.]   June 18, 1913

*   *   *   *   *   *   *

U.S. NAVAL OFFICER'S VIEW OF THE REVOLUTION
(<u>Confidential Report</u>)

The administration of President Francisco Madero had undoubtedly grown unpopular by February, 1913. Mr. Madero had been put into the presidency by the most fairly conducted election ever held in Mexico; though probably a bare ten per cent of the voting population had taken the trouble to go to the polls, Madero was virtually the unanimous choice of the nation.

A few months sufficed to show that the new President was unequal to the task to which he had been chosen. The ideals which he entertained in a generous heart could be applied, in a country that had all to learn of the meaning of "freedom" and "democracy," only with practical discretion; his promises of social, and particularly agrarian, reform could not be immediately realized; his most devoted supporters, once he was in power, revealed themselves in the character of self-seekers. Disillusioned, but confirmed in his belief that he had been called to a great mission, Madero adopted new methods--those, namely of repression. He bore down on the press, prescribed his enemies, gave his generals a free hand. But he was by nature unfitted to the part of a tyrant; a little man, of unimpressive presence and manner, highly nervous, overwhelmed by his troubles, surrounded by incompetents, trying to be severe but yielding, Madero, at the end of his first year in the presidency, was in a bad way. The country was to a considerable extent unsettled; murmuring was heard from every side; the treasury was depleted, and a gang of grafters scarcely less audacious than the hated Cientificos who had wrecked Porforio Diaz's rule were in the saddle. In a land of settled political methods the case would have been no worse than that of a particularly incompetent Chief Executive at the end of a disasterous first year. In Mexico, it was fairly certain that, unless an early change for the better came, a popular revolution might be expected. But the movement that broke out in the capital on the night of February 8 - 9 was in no sense a popular revolution. It was a conspiracy of army officers, financed by a few Spanish reactionaries, in conjunction with Cientifico exiles in Paris and Madrid.

Subscriptions towards the overthrow of Madero were passed around almost openly in the capital, with only moderate success, the principal amount used by the conspirators coming from abroad, in the shape of a draft for 12,000 pound sterling payable to the Bank of London and Mexico, Vera Cruz branch; it had been intended originally for Felix Diaz's uprising of last November. Leaders in the Mexican subscription were Gen. Luis Garcia Pimentel and Inigo Noreiga. Noreiga, sometimes referred to as "the Pierpont Morgan of Mexico" had been the recipient of many grants and monopolies from the old regime; he held Porfirio Diaz's power of attorney. The active agent of the plot was Gen. Manuel Mondragon, who had accumulated much money under Diaz as a fake artillery expert. He had been entrusted with many purchases of arms; the ingenious scheme of putting his name on "inventions" and collecting a royalty had been one of his methods. Mondragon corrupted the officers (old associates of his) and persuaded the cadets of the Asparantes military academy, at Tlalpam, a suburb of Mexico City, and they formed the nucleus of the movement.

On the night of February 8, a number of cadets came into the city, on trolley cars. In the early morning they gathered before the penitentiary, where they demanded the release of Gen. Felix Diaz, in confinement awaiting trial for rebellion. After a brief parley, Diaz was released. Then they proceeded to the Santiago military prison, where they demanded and secured the release of Gen. Bernardo Reyes, a prisoner in the like case with Diaz. President Madero, against the advise of his friends, had refused to permit Reyes and Diaz to be shot as traitors when captured, according to the prevailing Mexican custom, insisting that they be properly tried.

When released, General Reyes was found dressed in the full uniform of a general in the Mexican army, assumed while waiting for the doors to open for him. Mounting a horse, Reyes now led part of the cadets and a column of mutineering soldiers to the National Palace, in the center of the city, arriving there a little after eight o'clock Sunday morning. Reyes had full confidence that he would be welcomed and the Palace delivered over to him, the officers in command having been bribed. He rode up as if on parade. But in some way, the arrangement miscarried, and officers not in the plot were in charge Sunday morning. Reyes was fired on, and fell mortally wounded from his horse; the men behind him were routed, and many spectators were killed in the confused shooting that followed.

President Madero, receiving word in his palace of Chaupultepec, three miles away, about 9 o'clock mounted a horse and with a small escort rode into the city. Arriving at the end of the broad Avenida Juarez and finding the narrower streets thronged, he dismounted and went into a photographers studio opposite the unfinished National Theatre, to telephone for later news. Here he was joined by a few citizens and officers, among them Victoriano Huerta, a general in the army on leave for the treatment of his eyes. Huerta had been considered in disfavor and was known to be disappointed at not having been made Madero's Minister of War, the President knowing him to be an habitual drunkard. [Note: Capt. Barr, late U.S.A., now ordinance agent of the Bethlehem Steel Company, in Mexico, tells me Madero had given him this reason for not appointing Huerta, and that he had told Huerta, who said: "I know that was it."]

Huerta now offered his services to Madero. They were promptly accepted, and Huerta was appointed commander-in-chief of the army in the city. The commission was made formal on the following day.

The President stepped out on a balcony and made a speech to the crowd, Huerta standing by his side. He then went down, remounted his horse, a splendid animal that reared and plunged in the hands of the man who held him, commanded them to release him, and rode off, bowing to cheering crowds, alone, far ahead of his escort, to the National Palace.

General Diaz had been more successful than Reyes. Diaz's part had been to take possession of the arsenal, (the ciudadels) on the edge of the city. This he accomplished without opposition, and found himself in possession of a defensible fort, with the Government's reserve arms and ammunition. That evening Madero went to Cuernavaca, capital of the neighboring state of Morelos, where the army was operating against the bands of the rebel leader Zapata, and during the night brought back a train-load of arms and ammunition and some men. By Monday morning Madero had a garrison of one thousand in the National Palace.

On Monday neither side made any important move. The President had telegraphed to Gen. Aureliano Blanquet to move with his 1200 men from Tolusa, and had received word that the General was on the way.

On Tuesday, about 10 o'clock, the Government began the bombardment of the arsenal. The fire was vigorously replied to, and the city suffered severely. During the day, government re-enforcements (but not Blanquet's men) came in, and a supply of ammunition was received from Vera Cruz. There was no movement of the mutineers from the arsenal, and no evidence of disaffection in the city at large. The American Ambassador, however, on this day told all comers at the Embassy that the Government had practically fallen and telegraphed to Washington asking for powers to force the combatants to negotiations.

On the next day, Tuesday, February 12, the mutual bombardment continued. The Ambassador took the Spanish and German ministers and, as his report to the State Department that day shows, "protested against the continuance of hostilities." The President, continues Mr. Wilson's report, "was visibly embarrassed and endeavored to fix the responsibility of Felix Diaz."

The attitude of the American Ambassador towards President Madero had been one of undisguised contempt, from the beginning. Before the inauguration, at a dinner given Madero at the University Club in July, 1911, the Ambassador had publicly admonished the President-elect in terms of condescension that are still remembered by people of all classes in the city. Mr. Wilson boasted to me that on the very day of Madero's inauguration he had reported to Washington that the end was already in sight. When Felix Diaz rose in Vera Cruz, in November, 1912, Mr. Wilson, then in Kansas City, was quoted by the Associated Press as saying in an interview that Diaz was the type of man that ought to rule Mexico. Mr. Wilson repudiated the interview and denied using the language. As Madero's term went on, the Ambassador became more and more outspoken in the dislike of the President, his hostility to those who, even socially, consorted with him or his family and in predictions of his early fall.

The Ambassador now took the topsy-turvey view that the President, by not surrendering instantly to the mutineers, was responsible for the bloodshed. This view was congenial to the Spanish Minister, and to it were won the British and the German ministers. The Spanish and German ministers are not now in Mexico, but I have had the honour of meeting the British minister, and am obliged to say that I never met an individual whose character so absurdly belied his name. Mr. Stronge is a silly, stuttering imbecile, the laughing-stock of the whole city, which regales itself with nothing more to its perennial delight than daily stories of Mr. Stronge and the parrot by which he is constantly attended.

Mr. Wilson, in response to my questions, said to me that he called into consultation, on this and subsequent occasions, only his British, Spanish and German colleagues (with once perhaps the French charge) because they represented the largest interests here, and "the others really did not matter." At another time, Mr. Wilson explained to me that it would have been difficult to reach them all, so he consulted with those representing the largest interests.

The fact is, the others were not in accord with Mr. Wilson's policy. The Austrian and Japanese legations, with all the Latin-American representatives, including those of Brazil, Chile, Cuba, Guatemala and El Salvador, took the view that the constitutional government was justified in maintaining its authority, and that it was no business of foreign diplomatists to interfere against the constitutional government in a domestic conflict. Though Mr. Wilson constantly endeavors to represent his group as "the diplomatic corps," it is a fact that the numerical majority of the members of the corps acted in a contrary sense, under the Chilean and Cuban ministers.

Following the call on Madero during which Mr. Wilson, Mr. Stronge and Admiral von Hintze had told the President that they protested against his continuing hostilities, Mr. Wilson, accompanied by Mr. Stronge, went to the arsenal, called on Diaz, and as Mr. Wilson reports to Mr. Knox that day, "urged that firing be confined to a particular zone."

The Ambassador had thus reached the point where he admonished the legal Government as if it were a revolt, and treated the mutineers as if they were the Government de jure and de facto.

On Wednesday and Thursday, the 13th and 14th, the battle continued; the relative positions of the combatants remained unchanged, but distressing conditions increased in parts of the city within range of the fire. The Ambassador told Mr. Lascurain, Madero's prime minister and minister of foreign relations, that Madero ought to resign; as reported to Secretary Knox, Mr. Wilson's language became: "Public opinion, both Mexican and foreign, holds the Federal Government responsible for these conditions."

On Thursday, the 14th (although possibly on Wednesday the 13th) the United States Consul-General in Mexico City, Mr. Arnold Shanklin, who had been driven out of the consulate by artillery fire and was now doing heroic work at the Embassy, while busy in the yard in front of

the Embassy, was approached by a person of his acquaintance related
to General Huerta, who asked the favor of an introduction to the
Ambassador. He said:

"I have a message from the General; I believe it would be possible
to have him and Diaz come to an understanding, if the Ambassador
thinks that that would be a good idea. I want to see him and lay the
plan before him."

The messenger went on to explain that it would not be necessary
for the Ambassador to appear at all. He said that the interested parties
would be satisfied if Mr. Wilson were to authorize Mr. Shanklin to carry
on any negotiations and otherwise represent him. What they wanted was
an understanding with the Ambassador, without involving him in any
delicate responsibilities.

Mr. Shanklin replied that, so far as he was concerned, he would
have no part in any such plan; however, if the messenger insisted, he
would carry his request for an introduction to Mr. Wilson, and the
Ambassador could deal with it himself. Accordingly the Consul General
went in and informed the Ambassador of the messenger's request for an
introduction, explicitly stating the character of his errand, namely,
that he wanted to lay before the Ambassador a plan for an
understanding between the President's chief general and the rebel
leader. Mr. Shanklin explained that he had declined to have any part in
the matter, but that he deemed it his duty to lay it before the
Ambassador.

"Bring him in," said Mr. Wilson. "I want to see him." Mr.
Shanklin brought in the messenger, introduced him, and retired.

On Friday, the 15th, the Ambassador requested the British,
German and Spanish ministers to come to the embassy. He did not invite
the other members of the corps. He reports to Mr. Knox: "The opinion
of my assembled colleagues was unanimous." The Spanish minister was

designated to visit the National Palace and inform the President of this unanimous opinion - which was, that he should resign. Mr. Madero replied to the Spanish Minister that he did not recognize the right of diplomatists accredited to a nation to interfere in its domestic affairs; he called attention to the fact, which he feared some of the diplomatists had somehow overlooked, that he was the constitutional President of Mexico, and declared that his resignation would plunge the country into political chaos. He added that he might be killed, but he would not resign.

Later in the day, Mr. Wilson went to the Palace, accompanied by the German Minister. Their object, he says, was "to confer with General Huerta." But, he goes on, "upon arrival, much to our regret, we were taken to see the President." Huerta was called in, however, and an armistice was agreed on. Returning to the Embassy, the Ambassador sent the military attache to the arsenal to obtain, as he did, Diaz's consent to an armistice, over Sunday.

General Blanquet, with a regiment or two of men, arrived on Sunday, having taken a week to come forty miles, and it was soon apparent that they were not going into the fight.

Blanquet was betraying the President. So also was the man whom the President had made his commander-in-chief - Huerta.

Huerta had been in communications with Mr. Wilson, by means of the confidential messenger, and an understanding had been come to. During the armistice (ostensibly arranged for the burying of dead bodies and the removal of non-combatants from the danger zone), the details of the contemplated treachery were arranged, and before the close of the day Huerta sent word to Ambassador Wilson to that satisfactory effect. Mr. Wilson's report to the State Department that night contained the eupheumistic words: "Huerta has sent me a special messenger saying that he expected to take steps tonight towards terminating the situation."

The plot could not, for some reason, be carried out that night, but the messenger comes again on the morrow. This time, Mr. Wilson takes Mr. Knox a little more into his confidence: "Huerta has sent his messenger to say that I may expect some action which will remove Madero from power at any moment, and that plans were fully matured . . . I asked no questions and made no comment beyond requesting that no lives be taken - except by due process of law."

That night the Ambassador told at least one newspaper man that Madero would be arrested at noon on the morrow. Reporters were at the National Palace at the hour indicated, (at least one of them with dispatches written in advance ready for swift filing) but they were disappointed. Nothing occurred at the Palace at noon.

At the Gambrinus restaurant, however, that noon, the President's brother, Gustavo Madero, was arrested, after breakfasting with Huerta and other men, who, at the conclusion of the meal, seized him and held him prisoner. The plan of seizing the person of the President was delayed only an hour or so. At 2 o'clock, Mr. Wilson had the satisfaction of telegraphing to the State Department: "My confidential messenger with Huerta has just communicated [two words illegible] Madero's arrest.

"My confidential messenger with Huerta," "the confidential messenger between Huerta and myself, a person by whom the President has requested me to reach him whenever I desire," (Wilson to Knox Feb. 28) -- the anonymous figure which moves mysteriously in Wilson's reports and much more prominently in the true story of the Madero betrayal, was Enrique Zepeda, a notorious character who passes as the nephew and is the illegitimate son of Victoriano Huerta.

Enrique Zepeda is married to the step-daughter of an American, Mr. E.J. Pettegrew. Pettegrew says that on the Tuesday before the events now occurring, that is, on the first day of the battle, he and Zepeda arranged a meeting between Huerta and Diaz in an empty house in the city. If this is true, it would seem as if the whole bombardment were an elaborate fake, that the two generals understood each other all the time. Many other things point to this conclusion. It would then seem to be the case, if Pettegrew's story is true, that when Zepeda sought Mr. Wilson's offices to bring the two generals together, it was not because his intervention was necessary, but because the conspirations wanted to let the Ambassador believe that he was "solving the situation" and to secure his promise of Washington's recognition of the government they were plotting to set up. However, as I cannot substantiate this point fully, I disregard it entirely in the further narrative.

When Zepeda appeared at the embassy at 2 o'clock on the 18th, his hand was bleeding. He entered the basement, devoted to the offices of the secretaries and attaches, where were gathered a considerable number of people. Dr. Ryan, a Red Cross surgeon, was present, and immediately set about dressing Zepeda's hand, Mr. Shanklin holding it. Zepeda said: "I was shot helping arrest Madero, but I didn't stop to have anything done, because I had promised the Ambassador that he would be the first man told when we had done it." At this indiscretion, the group of onlookers were hastily dispersed and the doors closed.

A few minutes later, as the Ambassador was talking with Mr. E.S.A. de Lima, Manager of the Mexican Bank of Commerce (the Speyer bank) who was in the Embassy helping financially Americans in need of cash, -- they were at the top of the stairs leading from the basement, a clerk came up and said: "Mr. Ambassador, Mr. Zepeda says he must go off to carry a message to General Diaz, but his hand is bleeding a good deal and it is a pity he can't remain quietly here."

"Oh, yes," said Mr. Wilson, "he must not go out. Tell him he mustn't stir. I will see that his message is delivered. Tell Mr. Zepeda that I deeply appreciate all that he has done."

To break, here, a little away from the chronological arrangement of this story -- One day, a month later, Zepeda was telling the story of the arrest. Mr. C.A. Hamilton, an American mine owner of Oaxaca, broke in:

"If you people were going to do away with Madero, why in the world didn't you do it then, in the scuffle; it would have looked more natural."

"Why," replied Zepeda, "I had promised the Ambassador that we wouldn't kill him when we arrested him." This was on the evening of the 22nd of March at the house of J.N. Galbraith, in the hearing of Mr. Hamilton, Mr. Galbraith, Consul General Shanklin, all of whom have (separately) repeated the remark to me, and of Mr. C. R. Hudson.

Here as well as anywhere, Zepeda's history may be treated a little further:

As his reward for his services as a go-between, Zepeda was given the post of Governor of the Federal District. (He had lately been expelled from the Mexico Country Club for immorality in the club house.) On Sunday, March 9th he gave an elaborate dinner to Mr. Wilson and guests invited by the latter at the Chaupultepec Restaurant; on this occasion Mr. Wilson made a speech so savage in its denunciation of the Maderos and so frank in its avowal of his part in the overthrow and his delight in it that one of the party said to me, "We looked at each other in dismay, and some of us turned pale."

On the night of March 26, this man Zepeda, after dining with "President" Huerta and drinking afterward with a party in Sylvain's Restaurant, went to the prison in which was confined Gabriel Hernandez, general in the Mexican army, ordered him dragged into the patio, shot to death and his body burned. Petroleum was poured over the body, a match was applied. Zepeda watched the corpse slowly consumed, and then, with his companions, went to a house of prostitution, where he spent the rest of the night in unspeakably vile and cruel excesses such as he was already famous for.

"My confidential messenger with Huerta" is now in prison awaiting trial, but his release on the ground of insanity is expected.

On receipt of Zepeda's report, that Tuesday afternoon, Ambassador Wilson sent a message to Diaz at the arsenal, apprising him that the President had been arrested and that Huerta desired to confer with the rebel chieftain. It was agreed to hold the conference at the American Embassy. At 9 o'clock Huerta arrived at the embassy, and Mr. Wilson sent Doctor Ryan and others, in an automobile flying the American flag, for Diaz, who duly returned with the party. Mr. Wilson says the flag was not displayed on the return trip.

The leader of the mutiny, the traitorous commander-in-chief and the American Ambassador, with his translator, Luis d'Antin, spent the next three hours in conference in the smoking room of the embassy, framing up a plan for a new government to succeed that of the betrayed and imprisoned President. Diaz pressed his claims for the chief office, on the ground that he had fought the battle. But Huerta's claims were stronger, for, in truth, if he had not turned traitor, the revolt could not have succeeded. Three times they were on the verge of parting in anger, says the Ambassador, but his labors kept them together and finally worked out what was represented as a compromise: Huerta was to go in as Provisional President, but was to call an election and to support Diaz for the permanent presidency. A cabinet was agreed on, the Ambassador taking a leading part in this matter. He, for instance, put his vote on the naming of Vera Estanol as Minister of Foreign Relations, but consented to his going in as Minister of Education. When Zepeda was named for the governorship of the Federal District, the interpreter made a gesture of disgust, but was reproved by Mr. Wilson. The Ambassador says he stipulated for the release of Madero's ministers. He made no stipulation concerning the President and Vice President.

That night, within an hour of the adjournment of the conference at the embassy, Gustavo Madero; the President's brother, was driven into an empty lot just outside the arsenal, his body riddled with bullets and thrown into a hole in the ground.

On the following day, Francisco Madero, in imprisonment and threatened with death, at the pleading of his wife and mother, and, as she said, to save their lives, not his own, signed his resignation. Vice President Pino Suarez did the same.

The arrangement was that the resignations were to be placed in the hands of the Chilean and Cuban ministers for delivery only after the two retiring officials and their families were safely out of the country. It seems however to have been necessary for the documents to receive the authentication of the head of the cabinet, the Minister of Foreign Relations, and, while they were passing through his hands, such pressure was brought to bear upon Mr. Lascurain that he delivered the resignations directly and immediately into the hands of Madero's enemies.

Madero and Pino Suarez, however, had been promised release and safe-conduct for themselves and their families, out of the country. Mr. Wilson tells me that he had been consulted by Huerta as to the best methods of dealing with Madero - in particular, as to whether it would be better to deport Madero, or put him into an insane asylum. "I declined to express a preference," says the Ambassador. All I said was: 'General, do what you think is best for the welfare of Mexico,' Huerta decided, or pretended to decide, on deportation.

A train stood ready at the Mexican Railway station, to take Madero and Pino Suarez with their families down to Vera Cruz, where they were to go on board the Cuban gun-boat Cuba and be conveyed to a foreign shore. By nine o'clock the families hurriedly prepared for departure, were gathered, waiting, on the platform. The Chilean and Cuban Ministers, who had spent the day with Madero, had announced their intention of accompanying the party down to the port, and they appeared at the station, announcing that the President and Vice President would soon follow. They did not come. About midnight the Chilean Minister left the distressed women, hurried to the Palace, and asked to see General Huerta. The General sent out word that he was very tired after a hard day's work and was resting; he would see the Minister later. Mr. Riquelme waited until 2 o'clock and was still refused admittance to Huerta. He could do nothing but return to the station and advise the party to return to their homes.

In the morning it was explained that the military commandant of the port of Vera Cruz had received telegrams from Mrs. Madero which had led him to reply unsatisfactorily to Huerta's instructions. The commandante is said to have replied: "By whose authority? I recognize only the authority of the constitutional President of Mexico, Francisco I. Madero." It is the belief of Maderistas, however, that it was the decision of the Chilean and Cuban ministers to accompany the party that forbade the departure of the train, the plan having been to blow it up on the way down.

The wife and mother of Madero and relatives of Pino Suarez, relieved to learn that the men were still alive but fearing the worst, now appealed to the American Ambassador to grant the threatened men asylum in the embassy. He had opened it for a meeting-place of the plotting traitors, but he could not see his way to open it for their victims. Instead, Mr. Wilson recommended that they be transferred to more comfortable quarters -- from the Palace to the penitentiary. It is commonly understood that the women asked Mr. Wilson to transmit in American State Department cipher a message to the President of the United States, appealing for his influence toward saving the lives of the men. Of this and another incident which nevertheless I think it well to mention, I have no proof:

It is emphatically stated to me by the leader of the Madero sympathizers in the city, Serapio Rendon, that on the 20th the

American Ambassador received instructions from the State Department at Washington to inform General Huerta that improper treatment of the deposed President or Vice President would, in the opinion of the United States Government, have a most unfortunate effect, and that the Ambassador failed to communicate this message. I have no evidence that the charge is true, but Sr. Rendon's averment is so positively made that the matter merits investigation.

General Huerta assumed the presidency on the 20th, carefully observing certain formalities which are held to establish the legality of his rule. The President and Vice President having resigned, Madero's Minister of Foreign Relations was recognized as President for the few minutes necessary for him to appoint Victoriano Huerta Minister of Gobernation, and to resign, leaving Huerta to succeed, according to the Constitution, to the presidency.

On the 21st the American Ambassador telegraphed Secretary Knox that he would recognize the government thus set up and that he had already instructed all American consuls in the country to "urge general submission and adherence to the new government, which will be recognized by all foreign governments today."

The Ambassador appears to have received instructions from Mr. Knox not to accord this precipitate recognition, for later in the day he telegraphs that he had had an interview with the new minister of foreign relations, Mr. de la Barra, and trusts he has accomplished what the Department had in view, though he did "not resort to the refusal of full recognition."

(A reading of Mr. Wilson's dispatches to the Department during the next month shows him making reports of the progress of the new government and the submission to it of all parts of the country which are so exactly opposed to the truth as to be beyond all understanding. The fact is that from the moment of Huerta's accession the country began to fall rapidly under the sway of rebellion. Today Huerta is in control of less than half the country.)

The next day was Washington's Birthday. In the morning the Ambassador and the new Minister of Foreign Relations engaged in mutual felicitations before a crowd assembled at the Washington monument; after leaving wreaths on it, a march was made to the Juarez monument, where wreaths were also left. In the late afternoon, Mr. Wilson received at the embassy. The reception was attended by Huerta, Diaz, Mondragon and others of the new regime. Huerta and Wilson disappeared from the throng, and I have the authority of the Chilean Minister for the statement that Huerta and Wilson were engaged in conversation in the smoking-room, for an hour and a half -- during which time the Chilean Minister waited, having occasion to speak to Mr. Wilson. The Ambassador omits any mention of February 22 as one of the only dates in which he reports to Mr. Bryan (his long report of March 12) he had verbal or written communication with Huerta. The Chilean Minister may have been mistaken. If he be right we have Huerta and Wilson in conference up to 7 o'clock p.m.

At 9 o'clock, the warden of the penitentiary, was visited by Col. Luis Vallesteres with an order directing that the warden turn over the command of the prison to him. The retiring warden went to his home in the automobile that had brought his successor.

Very close upon the stroke of 12: that night, Francisco I. Madero and Jose Maria Pino Suarez were murdered. Ambassador Wilson reported to Washington the following morning that, as nearly as he could ascertain, they were killed as a result of an attempt at rescue as they were being transferred from the National Palace to the penitentiary. "I had recommended their transfer to more comfortable quarters", he explained. The story of the attempted rescue was abandoned, almost as soon as it was put out. Resort to the "ley fuga", with its legend against the names of victims "killed while attempting to escape", has been a favorite method for centuries in Spanish countries, but it has never been pretended as more than a convenient fiction.

As a matter of fact, Madero and Pino Suarez were put into two automobiles, one in each, at the Palace at 11:45, and were driven in the direction of the penitentiary, escorted by a dozen men, under the command of Major Francisco Cardenas. Cardenas, a particular comrade and henchman of Huerta, had reached the city only at 9 o'clock that night, coming from Manzanillo. The party did not go to the door of the penitentiary, but passed the street leading to it and went on to a vacant space back of the building. Here the automobile stopped. What occurred next will probably never be known exactly. According to the best evidence I have been able to gather, Pino Suarez was hauled out and shot. Then came the turn of Madero. A single bullet, in the back of the head, was his portion. The hair was singed. When the body was prepared for burial, a bruise was noticed in the forehead; it may have been result of his fall after the fatal shot or a blow by the pistol butt before it. The murderous band, their work done, swiftly disappeared. One of the automobiles had run off, the frightened driver never stopping for a shower of bullets. Soon afterward, a peon, with one companion, obscure prisoners, were sent by the new warden to bring the bodies in. [This peon] took from the pockets of the dead Vice-President a number of articles, which I have handled:

A sheet of paper bearing what is apparently a cipher code; a Kansas City, Mexico and Orient Railroad pass, No. 350; a Wells-Fargo Express frank, No. 3; an occulist's and an optician's prescription, and a draft, dated Mexico City 19 February, for $2000.00 U.S. Cy., in favor of Sr. Jose Maria Pino Suarez, signed by Salvador Madero y Cia. and addressed to Sr. Ed. Maurer, 80, Maiden Lane, New York City.

In the early morning, passers-by piled stones in a little mound over the two blood-soaked spots of ground and stuck lighted candles on top.

For several days following the assassination, Huerta and his Minister of Foreign Relations talked much of investigation. No investigation has been made. No investigation is under way. Major Cardenas was put under arrest, but was soon released, and promoted Lieutenant Colonel. He is now commanding rurales in Michoacan. Only the day before this paragraph is written, he figured in the papers as having shot a prisoner in cold blood.

Mr. Wilson has never made any demand for an investigation. In conversation with me, he exhibits no appreciation whatever of the nature of the deed done the night of February 22nd, after the entire group of men responsible for it had been guests at his house, no suspicion that any responsibility rested upon himself, who, in a sober view of the past, might be said to have delivered the men to death. Mr. Wilson bitterly vituperated Madero and his family, in conversation with me. He exhibits pride in the fact that he had consistently predicted Madero's fall. In reply to my question whether he thought he was in a proper diplomatic attitude in presiding at a conference of two revolting generals and in helping arrange the details of a new Presidency, when the constitutional President, to whom he was accredited, was held prisoner, the Ambassador replied that it was necessary for the good of Mexico that Madero be eliminated. To my question as to the responsibility for the death of Madero and Pino Suarez, Mr. Wilson said he took the ground that they were private citizens when they died, and that it would be an impertinence for a foreign power to demand an investigation into a purely domestic matter. He went on, with considerable violence, to say that Madero had killed hundreds illegally, and it was no concern of his how the man died. "In fact, the person really responsible for Madero's death was his wife. She was the one to blame. Madero had to be eliminated. By her telegram to Veracruz, she made it impossible to allow him to leave the Capital".

The above account of affairs in Mexico is made from the position that the movement against Madero was a conspiracy and not a popular revolution - a cuartelazo, a military coup, the plot of a few and not the

uprising of an outraged people; and that the betrayal of the President
by his generals was mercenary treachery and was not in the slightest
degree a response to the sentiments of a nation, or even of the city.

I have no reason to doubt - in fact, I believe - that Ambassador
Wilson was sincere in this opposite view. He undoubtedly thought that
the good of the country demanded the overthrow of Madero. He had
come to regard him as a Nero. Taking that view, a great deal can be
said in justification of many of Mr. Wilson's acts and in extenuation of
others. Taking that view, it is possible to tell the story in a very
different tone, with very different accents. Indeed, there are probably
omitted in this necessarily hurried story, a number of incidents that in
fairness ought to be told, on any theory.

Mr. Wilson, it is fair to say, talks freely and with every
appearance of candor of his part in the drama, and gives evidence in
every sentence that he believes it to have been the only part humanity
and patriotism (alike from the standpoint of Mexico and the United
States) allowed him to play. He is evidently surprised and deeply
disappointed that it is not so recognized by all. He is plainly puzzled
that the country at large has repudiated the revolution, which he holds
was undertaken and carried through in its behalf; deeply chagrined
that it did not bring about peace.

History will probably place the responsibility for the murder of
Madero elsewhere than on the shoulders of his faithful wife.
Nevertheless, curious as is this illustration of the length to which an
initial error can carry its victim, it is, in my judgment, absurd to
picture Mr. Wilson as a malicious plotter. The worse that can truthfully
be said is that, being a man of intense prejudices, he was so blinded
by his hatred of Madero, that he honestly mistook it for the hatred of
the whole Mexican people, his own conviction for the verdict of the
nation. None the less, however sincere may have been his motives, it is
impossible not to conclude that Mr. Wilson's course was utterly
mistaken, mischievous and tragically unhappy in its results.

It is hardly a matter of conjecture - it is a conclusion to which all facts point - that without the countenance of the American Ambassador given to Huerta's proposal to betray the President, the revolt would have failed. On Monday the 17th, the last day of the fighting, Madero was in undisputed possession of the entire city, except the arsenal and three or four houses near it still held as outposts. The mutineers had ventured on no sorties, and nothing whatever in the way of sympathy with them had appeared in any part of the city. The people had refused to rise. No sympathetic uprisings had occurred in the country. The Zapatistas, banditti long in possession of the State of Morelos and the mountains surrounding the city, had not come in, though Ambassador Wilson had daily telegraphed to Washington that they were coming. Instead, Zapata had sent word to Madero that they would suspend operations against the Federal Government until it had disposed of Felix Diaz. In brief, it was now, after a week, definitely ascertained that the Government had to do with nothing more than a single group of a few hundred man, surrounded and confined in a fort, the reduction of which was only a matter of time.

There was not a moment during the "Decena Tragica" when it would not have been possible to "end the distressing situation", "put a stop to this unnecessary bloodshed" by stern warning from the American Embassy to the traitorous army officers that the United States would countenance no methods but peaceful constitutional ones and recognize no government set up by force. President Madero was not betrayed and arrested by his officers until it had been ascertained that the American Ambassador had no objection to the performance. The plan for the immediate setting of a military dictatorship would never have been formed except in the American Embassy, under the patronage of the American Ambassador, and with his promise of his Government's prompt recognition. Madero would never have been assassinated had the American Ambassador made it thoroughly understood that the plot must stop short of murder.

It cannot but be a course of grief that what is probably the most dramatic story in which an American diplomatic officer has ever been involved, should be a story of sympathy with treason, perfidy and assassination in an assault on constitutional government. And it is particularly unfortunate that this should have taken place in a leading country of Latin America, where, if we have any moral work to do, it is to discourage violence and uphold law.

Trifling, perhaps, in the sum of miseries that have flowed from it, yet not without importance in a way, is the fact that thousands of Mexicans believe that the Ambassador acted on instructions from Washington and look upon his retention under the new American President as a mark of approval and blame the United States Government for the chaos into which the country has fallen.

Com. Bayard Hale

* * * * * * *

AMERICAN CONSULATE

Saltillo, Mexico
June 18th, 1913

SUBJECT: An account of incidents attendant upon the
capture of Concepcion del Oro by revolutionists
on May 20th, 1913. Political situation, Saltillo.

THE HONORABLE
THE SECRETARY OF STATE
WASHINGTON.

SIR:

The consulate is informed by Mr. P.E.O. Carr, Vice President and
General Manager of the Mazapil Copper Company and of the Coahuila
and Zacatecas Railway, that he finds himself and his companies in
marked disfavor with General Lopez, on account of the arrangements
made with the rebels concerning the Concepcion del Oro situation and
concerning the refugee train which came in to Saltillo from Concepcion
del Oro. The consulate understands that the General is of the opinion
that the rebels have made use of the railroad, the telegraph and the
telephone for their own purposes. The Department may recall an
intimation of such use mentioned in these despatches some time since.
Possibly for these reasons, and for others of his own, the General
issued an order to the railway company to tear up a section of its
track, as per the consulate's telegram of the 12th instant. When Mr.
Carr, the General Manager, declined to obey the order, some of the
rails were removed, and the telegraph and telephone lines were cut,
with instruction to make no repairs. Since that time, there has been no
communication whatever with Concepcion. Four foreign employees of the

company, among them one American, who had come in on the refugee train, undertook to go back to Concepcion, by hand car, walking when they could not use it. It was a most rash attempt. The General heard of it just after they had left town, and sent an orderly with an urgent message to Mr. Carr, informing him that the federal outposts had orders to fire at once on any one attempting to pass the lines. The same Edward L. Degoner, who was falsely reported to the Department as being under sentence of death, made a furious ride on horseback and overtook the travelers before they had gotten into danger. It is a current opinion among foreigners who are aware of all the circumstances, that the General doubtless feels some chagrin over the entire Concepcion del Oro affair, and that he will possibly endeavor to, as far as he can, shift his own responsibility onto the Mazapil Copper Company and the Coahuila and Zacatecas Railway, who are in fact, the chief sufferers.

The consulate's telegram of the 12th mentioned that the rebels were evacuating Concepcion, that some apprehension was felt here and that developments might be expected. At five o'clock on the afternoon of the 13th, the consulate wired the Consul General as follows: "Rebels are reported between Saltillo and Monterey. Eleven bridges are reported burned between Monterey and Reata." This message was sent in code. At the time it was sent, neither the Embassy nor the Department could be reached. The same night, the station at Santa Maria, thirteen miles North of Saltillo, was burned and track destroyed, suspending railway communication with Monterey. Thus confirming the consulate's surmise in the closing clause of despatch No. 195, of the 9th instant, and the intimation terminating the telegram of the 12th.

The federal wire continued working to Monterey only. Late in the evening of Saturday, the 14th, the following message was sent, in code, to the Consul General: "Repairs on bridges and track destroyed North of Ramos Arzipe will be undertaken tomorrow. Federals retreated from advanced position south of Monelova. Their situation is critical. Embassy unadvised." By Monday, the 16th, the track had been repaired and the train from Monterey arrived. The Department and Embassy were reached by special permission of General Lopez, and both were notified of the restoration of railway communication with Monterey.

The consulate takes this opportunity to say that for several days it has been extremely difficult, and, at times, impossible, to get service over the federal wire for commercial or private telegrams. A few messages have been received, but when replies are presented for transmission, the public is simply told that there is no communication, or that the line is not now working. Though having special permission to transmit official telegrams whenever the General himself can transmit his own, the consulate has had various official telegrams returned, with a statement to the messenger that there was no communication. When the Vice Consul presented the same telegrams in person, they were received on condition of their being transmitted as urgent, and the extra price (double) paid; some thin pretext being offered for not accepting the telegram from the consulate's [one word unintelligible]

The consulate's telegram of the 16th, also informed the Department that on Sunday night, the 15th, the neighboring mountain village of Arteaga was looted. This work was done by Francisco Coss. General Pena was sent in pursuit. It has been difficult to get the facts of this expedition. It was given out as a federal triumph. It is also reported that the federals were decoyed up into a canyon by Coss, and that they lost a number of men. One known fact is that they returned to Saltillo and the town was immediately occupied again by the rebels; and the rebels are still in possession. These same people made a daring raid into the Eastern suburbs of Saltillo this morning at three o'clock, causing great alarm and commotion. Between rebels and federals, it is estimated that as many as a thousand shots were fired during the half hour of the raid. It was stated that two rebels paid with their lives for this rashness, but the consulate could get no positive confirmation, and doubts the statement. The incident was reported to the Department in the telegram of one o'clock this afternoon.

In the consulate's telegram of the 16th, the Department was informed that the federals had retreated from their advanced position South of Monelova. At that time it was understood that the column had been lessened until it consisted of only about four hundred men and that they had fallen back to Espinazo, fortified themselves there, and that their situation was critical, as rebels from Monelova and Candela (Romero Rubio), were approaching. This information was given to the consulate by a Mexican conductor, who had just brought in the supply train from Espinazo. The consulate has heard nothing further from these troops, but it is believed that they have retreated still farther South, possibly as far as Paredon; and it is known that they are to be called in to Saltillo, if they are needed here. It is reported that as the federals have retreated, rebels from Monelova have slowly followed them destroying again the railroad that the federals had repaired.

Among the passengers who came in on the first train from Monterey, was Dr. J. F. Moore, a well known member of the American colony in Saltillo. He had arrived in Monterey at three o'clock that same morning from a very adventurous trip through the country from Laredo to Monterey by automobile. Being personally acquainted with Don Venustiano, he had made a special trip from San Antonio to Eagle Pass to get a passport from him for use in case of a holdup by the constitutionalists. To the Doctors surprise, this was rather brusquely declined, and he was informed that his proposed trip was not approved. He was not molested by the rebels, however, as he avoided the places where they were known to be. He had some trouble after reaching the federal lines, and came near being detained and having the machine confiscated. He is the first American who has made the trip through from Laredo to Saltillo, in many weeks. He reports that the large iron bridge near Villaldama, North, has been dynamited; and while the structure is not destroyed, it is out of position. Doctor Moore also told the consulate in confidence, that he personally counted twenty eight dead federals lying in the highway where they had fallen in battle, and was told of five others just off the road. These were still remaining grewsome, unburied witnesses of the recent encounter at Bustamante heralded as a glorious federal victory.

Mr. A. L. Dyer, another well known member of the Saltillo American colony, was also a passenger on the train from Monterey. He had tried to come through from San Luis to Saltillo, expecting to work his way as best he could from Vanegas. He found the trip entirely impracticable on account of the presence of rebels in considerable numbers in the vicinity of Vanegas, and Northward. From two Mexican railroad men who had walked through from Saltillo, to join their families in San Luis, he heard that the rebels had been employing the section men to destroy the track by unbolting the rails, making piles of the crossties, placing the rails on the piles and then setting the piles on fire.

From persons who have recently called at the consulate from Parras, the consulate learns that the large industries at that place in which the Madero family is concerned, have been closed down. The town has been in undisturbed possession of the rebels for months.

At one o'clock this afternoon the Department, the Embassy and the Consulate General were advised of the near approach to Saltillo, of a large body of revolutionists. Their main position is at Agua Nueva, twenty miles South. These are the same people who have recently been at Concepcion del Oro. Their number is placed at something more than two thousand, and they evidently intend to attack this city. Their scouts have approached as near as Buena Vista, seven miles South. As above stated, Coss continues to occupy Arbeaga, ten miles East. His force is said to be from three to five hundred men. The city has been in quite a panic all the afternoon, and the General has begun his preparations for defense. He has about one thousand men, some artillery and an abundance of ammunition. He has very little cavalry but feels entirely confident that he can protect the city against any attack the rebels may make. Late in the afternoon the armored automobile making the round of the principal streets, drew up in front of the consulate and proceeded to wire the streets leading North and East. The following message was sent the Consul General: "Streets now being barb wired. Attack expected tonight."

I have the honor to be, Sir
Your obedient servant,

John R. Silliman
Vice Consul in Charge

*   *   *   *   *   *   *

226 FIFTH AVENUE
NEW YORK

June 21, 1913

Dear Secretary Bryan,

Since you appeared interested in the personalities of Generals
Huerta and Felix Diaz in Mexico, I take pleasure in sending you the
drafts of two biographical articles concerning these two gentlemen.

You may be interested to know that the enclosed despatch to the
N.Y. Times, which you may have seen, was furnished to the Times by
Mr. Paul Hudson. As I told you this gentleman has come to Washington
purely as an agent of the present Mexican government. When I saw him
last, a few days ago, he showed me a long cablegram of instructions
sent him by Don Francisco de la Barra, from the Mexican Foreign
Office.

Very sincerely yours,

Edwin Emerson

VICTORIANO HUERTA

by Edwin Emerson

There is a saying in Mexico that it is much easier to be a general than a peaceful president. Inasmuch as almost all Mexican presidents, during the hundred years since Mexico became a Republic, got into the presidency by force of arms, this saying is significant. At all events no Mexican general, who won his way into the National Palace by his military prowess, ever won his way out with credit to himself or to his country since the early days of General Guadelupe Victoria, Mexico's first President.

General Victoriano Huerta, Mexico's latest Interim-President, immediately after his overthrow of the Madero government found out to his own cost how much harder it is to rule a people than an army.

As a matter of fact, though, General Huerta was boosted into his interim presidency before he really had a fair opportunity to learn how to lead an army. At the time he was so suddenly made Chief Magistrate of Mexico he was not commanding the Mexican army, but was merely a recently appointed major general who happened to be in command of that small fraction of the regular army at the capital, which was supposed to have remained loyal to President Madero and his constitutional government. Huerta had been appointed by President Madero to the supreme command of the loyal forces at the capital, numbering barely three thousand soldiers, only a few days before Madero's fall. Even if he had not turned traitor to his Commander-in-Chief, as he did in the end, Huerta's command of the loyal troops during the ten days' struggle at the capital preceding the fall of the constitutional government, could not be described as anything but a dismal failure.

Before considering General Huerta's qualifications as a President, one should know something of his career as a soldier. During the last few years it has repeatedly fallen to my lot to follow General Huerta in the field, so that I have had a fair chance to view some of his soldiery qualities at close hand. I accompanied General Huerta during his campaign through Chihuahua, in 1912, and was present at his famous Battle of Bachimba, near Chihuahua City, on July 3d, 1912, - the one decisive victory won by General Huerta against the rebel forces of Pascual Orozco. Before this campaign, I was in Cuernavaca in the State of Morelos, during the time when General Huerta had his headquarters there in his campaign against Zapata's bandit hordes in that State after the fall of General Diaz' government. While Porfirio Diaz was still President I received permission from him to accompany General Huerta's troops into Morelos, for the first campaign against Zapata, but we had got no farther than Cuernavaca, where the military railway stopped, before the campaign came to an ignominious end, - General Huerta being recalled to the capital. We had barely got back to Mexico City when the Diaz government went out of existence.

General Huerta then took charge of the last military escort which accompanied General Porfirio Diaz on his midnight flight from Mexico City to the port of Veracruz. During the ten hours' run down to the coast, it may be recalled, the train on which President Diaz and his family rode was held up by rebels in the grey of dawn, and the soldiers of the military escort had to deploy in skirmish order, led by Generals Diaz and Huerta in person: but the affair was over after a few minutes firing, with no casualties on either side. Afterward the rebels sent in a written apology for their "mistake."

Before this eventful year General Huerta had but few opportunities of winning laurels on the field of battle. Having entered the Military Academy of Chapultepec in the early seventies under Lerdo de Tejada's presidency, Victoriano Huerta was graduated in 1875, at the age of 21, and was commissioned a second lieutenant of engineers. While still a cadet at Chapultepec he showed predilection for scientific subjects, particularly mathematics and astronomy. During the military rebellion of Oaxaca, when General Diaz rose against President Lerdo, Lieutenant

Huerta was engaged in garrison duty and got no opportunity to enter this campaign.

After General Diaz had come into power and had begun his reorganization of the Mexican army, young Huerta, lately promoted to a captaincy of engineers, came forward with a plan for organizing a General Staff. General Diaz approved of his plans and Captain Huerta, accordingly, in 1879, became the founder of Mexico's present General Staff Corps. The first work of the new General Staff was to undertake the drawing up of a military map of Mexico on a large scale. The earliest sections of this immense map, on which the Mexican General Staff is still hard at work, were surveyed and drawn up in the State of Veracruz, where the Mexican Military Map Commission still has its headquarters. Captain Huerta accompanied the commission to Jalapa, the capital of the State of Veracruz, and served there through a period of eight years, receiving his promotion to major in 1880 and to Lieutenant Colonel in 1884. During this time he had charge of all the astronomical work of the Commission and he also led surveying and exploring parties over the rough, mountainous region that extends between the cities of Jalapa and Orizaba. While at Jalapa he married Emilia Aguila, of Mexico City, who bore him three sons and two daughters.

In 1890 Huerta was promoted to a colonelcy and was recalled to Mexico City where he remained with the General Staff for ten years, in practical direction of its topographical and astronomical departments. In 1901 he left the General Staff and was ordered to Sonora to command part of the infantry in the campaign against the Yaqui Indians of that year. After the campaign was over, Colonel Huerta again was put in charge of the General Staff's topographical work in Sonora and succeeded in mapping the central portion of that mountainous State, before another Yaqui war put an end to this work.

So soon as the Yaqui Indians had once more been subdued, Colonel Huerta was ordered to Yucatan to command part of the regular infantry there in the campaign against the Maya Indians. There he served several years until the last of the hostile Mayas had been deported to the jungles of Quintana Roo.

As a reward for his Indian campaign services Huerta was promoted to the rank of brigadier general and was once more detailed to the General Staff at the Capital. In Mexico's centennial year of 1910, when Francisco I. Madero rose in the north, and other parts of the Republic gave signs of disaffection, General Huerta was ordered south to take charge of all the detached government forces in the mountainous State of Guerrero. Almost simultaneously with his arrival in Chilpancingo, the capital of the State of Guerrero, though, almost the whole south of Mexico rose in rebellion. The military situation there was soon found to be so hopeless that Huerta was recalled to Mexico City for the purpose of organizing a strong military expedition against Guerrero.

I was in the capital at this time and took a lively interest in these military preparations, having received an official assignment to General Huerta's "Army of Guerrero" as war correspondent. The real "Army of Guerrero", however, was the army of rebels that was organized in that State under the leadership of the Figueroa brothers; and long before Huerta had made any headway in organizing his corps of regulars, the whole State of Guerrero except the military port of Acapulco, was lost to the government. There was no quick way of getting into Guerrero because all the lines of communication were held by the rebels; moreover the rebels, marching in three separate columns led by Ambrosio Figueroa, Juan Andrew Almazan and Jesus Salgado, were pouring into the neighboring State of Morelos, where Emiliano Zapata had just raised his banner of revolt, only a few days' march from the Capital.

So it was decided that Huerta should lead his mixed column of infantry, cavalry and artillery into Morelos, rather than into distant Guerrero.

There was talk of sending 10,000 men, and for a fortnight or more the wide stairways and corridors of the Mexican War Department, - then under the direction of old General Cosio, - were thronged with officers expecting marching orders. Then it was announced that the column was to be reduced to eight thousand men, and presently to seventy-five hundred men. When Huerta's expedition finally got away, after infinite bustle and preparation, one mixed train of forty cars carried all the men, animals, guns and ammunition. The whole column did not number more than 600 men at the utmost. I doubt whether it would have been dispatched to the front so soon, had it not been for a sensational train hold-up and murder of an American passenger by Zapatista bandits on the line between the Capital and Cuernavaca three days before.

General Huerta's column had barely detrained and moved into the military barracks at Cuernavaca, when it was announced that another body of federals was hemmed in by the rebels at Cusutla in Morelos not more than two marches away. I expected General Huerta to march to the relief of these soldiers, but no marching orders were issued, and presently the federal survivors of the Cuautla garrison came straggling into Cuernavaca in small detached groups, telling blood-curdling stories of a ferocious massacre of their comrades after a formal surrender of Cuautla. The people of Cuernavaca became highly excited and looked to General Huerta for a vigorous counter movement against the victorious rebels, known to be closing in on Cuernavaca, but again the soldiers under his command were not called upon to do anything but their old sleepy round of garrison duty. Within a week General Huerta was recalled to Mexico City and returned at once, accompanied by his staff, as well as by his artillery and machine guns.

Cuernavaca soon afterward was surrendered to the rebels without a shot being fired. I was there when Zapata made his triumphal entry into the city with all his men, followed by an abject rear guard of disarmed and dismounted federal soldiers, the remnants of Huerta's relief column and of the original federal garrison.

After General Huerta saw General Porfirio Diaz off to Europe at Veracruz he returned to the Capital and placed himself at the disposition of Don Francisco L. de la Barra, Mexico's new President ad interim. President de la Barra was at a loss what to do with him, until, a few weeks later, it became clear that Madero's plan of paying money to the former rebels and bandits in Morelos to persuade them to be good and keep the peace was having just the opposite effect. Then President de la Barra dispatched General Huerta with another column of soldiers to Cuernavaca to restore order. At the same time Senor Madero, then still a private citizen, offered to go to Cuernavaca to see what he could do as a mediator. General Huerta was very annoyed at this.

When Madero arrived at Cuernavaca and Huerta learned that Madero was stopping at the house of the State governor, Huerta at his headquarters in the Hotel Bellavista angrily pounded his fist on the table where he was drinking cognac and explained: "Madero need not expect me to come to him to pay my respects. I do not recognize his right to interfere here. If he wants to mediate between the government and the rebels, he will have to come to me first, for permission." One hour after this angry speech General Huerta, accompanied by his staff in gala uniform, called at the governor's house "to pay his respects to Senor Madero," and in the interview which followed, he placed himself "at Senor Madero's disposition."

Madero told Huerta to remain quiet with his troops at Cuernavaca until Madero should have had an opportunity to visit Zapata and his brother chieftains at their rebel camp in Cuautla, several days' ride away. General Huerta promptly agreed to this.

As it turned out, though, it took so long for Madero to reach Zapata in Cuautla, and to be heard from that Huerta grew impatient and, professing to entertain fears for Madero's safety, marched his men out of Cuernavaca in the direction of Cuautla, thus threatening immediate frustration of the peace negotiations. Madero got wind of this and promptly telephoned Huerta to stop his march. At the same time Madero telegraphed to President de la Barra at Mexico City to order Huerta back to Cuernavaca, pending Madero's peace parleys at Cuautla. The upshot was that Huerta and his column returned to Cuernavaca.

Huerta never forgave Madero for this. This did not prevent him, though, from continuing his service in the army and from placing himself at Senor Madero's complete disposition, when the latter was elected and inaugurated as President of Mexico. Madero, for reasons that are self-evident, was anxious to propitiate the military element, and to secure the cooperation of the more experienced officers in the regular army for the better pacification of the country. Accordingly, when Zapata and his bandit hordes gave signs of returning to their old ways, refusing to "stay bought", President Madero sent General Huerta back into Morelos, at the head of a strong force of cavalry, mountain artillery and machine guns, numbering altogether 3,500 men, with orders to put down Zapata's new rebellion "at any cost." At the same time President Madero induced his former fellow-rebel, Ambrosio Figueroa, now Commander-in-Chief of Mexico's rural guards, to cooperate with General Huerta by bringing a mounted force of three thousand rurales from Guerrero into Morelos from the south so as to hem in the Zapatistas between himself and Huerta at Cuernavaca. Figueroa's men, though they had to cover three times the distance, struck the main body of the rebels first and got badly mussed up in the battle that followed. General Huerta's column did not get away from Cuernavaca until the second day of the fight, and did not reach the battle-field in the extinct crater of Mount Herradura until Figueroa's rurales had been all but routed. In the battle that followed General Huerta succeeded in driving the rebels out of their strong position, but the losses of the federals, owing to their belated arrival and hastily taken positions, were disproportionately heavy.

This affair caused much ill feeling between the rurales and regulars, and Figueroa sent word to Madero that he could not afford to sacrifice his men by trying to cooperate with such a poor general as

Huerta. The much-heralded joint campaign accordingly fell to the ground.

President Madero **thereupon** recalled General Huerta and sent General Robles, of the regular army, to replace him in command. This furnished Huerta with another grievance against Madero.

Some time afterward I heard General Huerta explain in private conversation to some of his old army comrades that he had been recalled from Morelos because of his sharp military measures against the Zapatistas, owing to President Madero's sentimental preference for dealing leniently with his old Zapatista friends. At the time when General Huerta made this private complaint, however, it was a notorious fact that his successor in Morelos, General Robles, had received public instructions from Madero to deal more severely with the Morelos rebels. General Robles, as a matter of fact, handled the Morelos rebels far more ruthlessly than Huerta, leading to his own subsequent recall on charges of excessive cruelty.

Meanwhile the Orozco rebellion had arisen in the north, and became so threatening **that** General Gonzalez Salas, Madero's War Minister, felt called upon to resign his portfolio to take the field against Orozco, together with Generals Blanquet, Trucy Aubert and Tellez. General Gonzalez Salas, after organizing a fairly formidable looking force of 3,500 regulars and three batteries of field artillery at Torreon, rushed into the fray only to suffer a disgraceful defeat in his first battle at Rellano, in Chihuahua, not far from Torreon. General Gonzalez Salas took his defeat so much to heart that he committed suicide on his way back to Torreon. This, together with the panic stricken return of his army to Torreon, caused the greatest dismay at the Capital, the inhabitants of which already believed themselves threatened by an irresistible advance of Orozco's rebel followers. None of the federal generals at the front were considered strong enough to stem the tide.

The only available federal general of high rank, who had any experience in commanding large forces in the field, was Victoriano Huerta. President Madero in his extremity called upon General Huerta to reorganize the badly disordered forces at Torreon and to take the field against Orozco, "cost what it may." This was toward the end of March, 1912.

General Huerta, whom the army had come to regard as "shelved", lost no time in getting to Torreon. There he soon found that the situation was by no means so black as it had been painted. General Trucy Aubert, who had been cut off with one of the columns of the army, having cleverly extricated his force from its dangerous predicament so as to bring it safely back to the base at Torreon without undue loss of men or prestige.

Thenceforth no expense was saved by General Huerta in bringing the army to better fighting efficiency. Heavy reinforcements of regulars, especially of field artillery, were rushed to Torreon from the Capital and large bodies of volunteers and irregulars were sent after them from all parts of the Republic.

President Madero had said: "Let is cost what it may"; so all the preparation went forward regardless of cost. "Hang the expense!" became the blithe motto of the army.

When General Huerta at last took the field against Orozco, early in May, his federal army, now swelled to more than six thousand men and twelve pieces of artillery, moved to the front in a column of eleven long railway trains, each numbering from forty to sixty cars, loaded down with army supplies and munitions of all kinds, besides a horde of several thousand camp followers, women, [one word unintelligible] and other non-combatants. The entire column stretched over a distance of more than four miles. The transportation and sustenance of this unwieldy column, which had to carry its own supply of drinking water, it was estimated, cost the Mexican government nearly 350,000 pesos per day. Its progress was exasperatingly slow owing to the fact that the Mexican Central Railway, which was Huerta's only chosen line of advance, had to be repaired almost rail by rail.

After more than a fortnight's slow progress, General Huerta struck Orozco's forces at Conejos, in Chihuahua, near the branch line running out to the American mines at Mapimi. Orozco's forces, finding themselves heavily outnumbered and overmatched in artillery, hastily evacuated Conejos, retreating northward up the railway line by means of some half dozen railway trains. Several weeks more passed before Huerta again struck Orozco's forces at Rellano in Chihuahua, close to the former battlefield, along the railway, where his predecessor, General Gonzalez Salas, had come to grief. This was in June.

Huerta, with nearly twice as many men and three times as much artillery, drove Orozco back along the line of the railway after two days' long-range artillery bombardment, against which the rebels were powerless. This battle, in which the combined losses in dead and wounded on both sides were less than 200, was described in General Huerta's official report as "more terrific than any battle that had been fought in the western hemisphere during the last fifty years." In his last triumphant bulletin from the field General Huerta telegraphed to President Madero that his brave men had driven the enemy from the heights with a final fierce bayonet charge, and that their bugle blasts of victory could be heard even then on the crest.

Pascual Orozco, on the other hand, reported to the revolutionary Junta in El Paso, that he had ordered his men to retire before the superior force of the federals, and that they had accomplished this without disorder by the simple process of boarding their waiting trains and steaming slowly off to the north, destroying the bridges and culverts behind them as they went along. One of my fellow war correspondents, who served on the rebel side during this battle, afterward told me that the federals, whose bugle calls Huerta heard on the heights, did not get up to this position until two days after the rebels had abandoned their trenches along the crest.

The subsequent advance of the federals from Rellano to the town of Jimenez, Orozco's old headquarters, which had been evacuated by him without firing a shot, lasted another week.

Here Huerta's army camped for another week. At Jimenez the long brewing unpleasantness between Huerta's regular officers and some of Madero's bandit friends, commanding forces of irregular cavalry, came to a head. The most noted of these former guerrilla chieftains was Francisco Villa, an old time bandit, who now rejoiced in the honorary rank of colonel. Villa had appropriated a splendid Arab stallion, originally imported by a Spanish horse breeder with a ranch near Chihuahua City. General Huerta coveted this horse, and one day, after an unusually lively carouse at general headquarters, he sent a squad of soldiers to bring the horse out of Villa's corral to his own stable. The old bandit took offense at this and came stalking into headquarters to made a personal remonstrance. He was put under arrest and Huerta forthwith sentenced him to be shot. That same day the sentence was to be put into execution. Villa was already facing the firing squad, and the officer in charge had given the command to load, when President Madero's brother Emilio, who was serving on Huerta's staff in an advisory capacity, put a stop to the execution by taking Villa under his personal protection. President Madero was telegraphed to and immediately replied, reprieving Villa's sentence and ordering him to be sent to Mexico City pending further official investigation.

This act of interference infuriated Huerta. For the moment he had to content himself with formulating a long string of serious charges against Villa, ranging from military insubordination to burglary, highway robbery and rape. It was given out at headquarters that Villa had struck his commanding general.

Huerta never forgave the Madero brothers for their part in this affair, and his resentment was fanned to white heat, subsequently, when Francisco Villa was allowed to escape scot free from his prison in Mexico City.

At length the camp at Jimenez, which had grown exceedingly dirty and unhealthy, was broken up, and Huerta resumed his slow advance northward along the railway line. Inasmuch as the rebels retreated just as steadily and slowly as the federals advanced, without attempting any real show of resistance, there was no more fighting for several weeks. The so-called campaign settled down to a mere contest of railroad destruction on one side and railroad reconstruction on the other. Whenever a railroad station with a water tank was reached on the Chihuahua desert, the federal army halted for a comfortable rest of three or four days, or more, leaving the rebels some five or six miles ahead, beyond the customary gap of burnt bridges and torn up rails, to enjoy their leisure in their own way.

Meanwhile Huerta kept telegraphing to President Madero for more reinforcements of men, munitions and supplies, more engines, more railway trains and tank cars, and above all for more artillery. Madero kept sending them, though it cost his government a new loan of forty million dollars. Every other day or so a new train with fresh supplies arrived at the front.

At the end of several more weeks, when Orozco had slowly retreated half way through the State of Chihuahua, and when he found that the destruction of the big seven-span railway bridge over the Conchos River at Santa Rosalia did not permanently stop Huerta's advance, he reluctantly decided to make another stand at the deep cut of Bachimba, just south of Chihuahua City. This was in July.

By this time General Huerta's federal column had swelled to 7,500 fighting men, 20 pieces of field artillery, 30 machine guns and some 7,500 camp followers and women, making a total of more than 15,000 persons of all sexes and ages, who were being carried along on more than twenty railroad trains, stretching over a dozen miles of single track. The column was so long that some of my companions and I, when we climbed a high hill near the front end of the column at Bachimba, found it impossible to discern the tail end through our field glasses. All the hungry people that were being carried on all those twenty railroad trains, had to be fed, of course; so that none of us were surprised to read in the Mexican newspapers that the Chihuahua campaign was now costing Madero's government nearly 500,000 pesos per day.

The battle at Bachimba must have been swelled this budget. During this one day's fight nearly two million rifle cartridges and more than 10,000 artillery projectiles were fired away by the federals. Huerta's twenty pieces of field artillery, neatly posted in a straight line on the open plain, barely half a mile away from his ammunition railway train, kept firing at the supposed rebel positions all day long without any appreciable interruption, and all day long the artillery caissons and limbers kept trotting to and fro between the batteries and ammunition cars. Orozco had but 3,000 men with two pieces of so-called artillery, with gun barrels improvised from railroad axles, so he once more ordered a general retreat by way of his railroad trains, waiting at a convenient distance on a bend of the road behind the intervening hills. As at Rellano, at Conejos and at other places in the campaign where the railroad swept in big bends around the hills, no attempt was made on the federal side to cut off the rebels' retreat by short cut flanking movements of cavalry, of which Huerta had more than he could conveniently use, or chose to use. The whole ten hours' bombardment and rifle fire resulted in but fourteen dead rebels; but it won the campaign for the government and earned for Huerta his promotion to major general besides the proud title of "Hero of Bachimba."

President Madero and his anxious government associates were more than glad to receive the tidings of this "decisive victory." The only trouble was that it did not decide anything in particular. Orozco and his followers, while evacuating the capital of Chihuahua, kept on wrecking railway property between Chihuahua City and Juarez, and the campaign kept growing more expensive every day.

It took Huerta from July until August to work his slow way from the center of Chihuahua to Ciudad Juarez on the northern frontier. Before he reached his goal, though, the rebels had split into many smaller detachments, some of which cut his communications in the rear, while other harried his flanks with guerrilla tactics and threatened to carry the "war" into the neighboring State of Sonora. So far as the trouble and expense to the federal government was concerned this guerrilla warfare was far more than the preceding slow, but sure, railway campaign.

General Huerta himself, who was threatened with the loss of his eyesight from cataract, gave up trying to pursue the fleeing rebel detachments in person, but kept close to his comfortable headquarters in Ciudad Juarez and Chihuahua City. This unsatisfactory condition of affairs gave promise of enduring indefinitely, until President Madero in Mexico City, whose government had to bear the financial brunt of it all, suddenly lost his patience and recalled Huerta to the Capital, leaving the command in General Rabago's hands.

For reasons that were never quite fathomed by Madero's government, Huerta took his time about obeying these orders. Thus he lingered first at Ciudad Juarez, then at Chihuahua City, then at Santa Rosalia, next at Jimenez, and presently at Torreon, where he remained for over a week, apparently sulking in his tent like Achilles. This gave rise to grave suspicions, and rumors flew all over Mexico that Huerta was about to make common cause with Orozco. President Madero himself, at this time, told a friend of mine that he was afraid Huerta was going to turn traitor. About the same time, at a diplomatic reception, President Madero stated openly to Ambassador Wilson that he had reasons to suspect Huerta's loyalty. At length, however, General Huerta appeared at the Capital and, after a somewhat chilly interview with the President, obtained a suspension from duty so that he might have his eyes treated by a specialist.

Thus it happened that Huerta, who was nearly blind then, escaped being drawn into the sudden military movements that grew out of General Felix Diaz' unexpected revolt and temporary capture of the port of Veracruz, last October.

General Huerta's part in Feliz Diaz' second revolution, four months later, is too recent to have been forgotten. He was the senior ranking general at the Capital when the rebellion broke out and was summoned to his post of duty by President Madero from the very first. He accompanied Madero in his celebrated ride from Chapultepec Castle to the National Palace on the morning of the first day of the famous "Ten Days" and was put in supreme command of the forces of the government after the first hurried council of war. President Madero, totally lacking in military professional knowledge as he was, confided the entire conduct of the necessary war measures to General Huerta; but it soon became apparent that the old general either could not or would not direct any energetic offensive movement against the rebels. From the very first the government committed the fatal blunder of letting the rebels slowly proceed to the Citadel, - a fortified military arsenal, the retention of which was of paramount importance. Later, when it became clear that the rebels could not be dislodged from this stronghold by street rushes, no attempt was made to shell them out of their strong position by a high-angle bombardment of plunging explosive shells.

After it was all over General Huerta explained the ill success of his military measures during the ten days' street fighting by saying that President Madero was a madman who had spoiled all Huerta's military plans and measures by utterly impracticable counter orders. At the time, though, it was given out officially that Huerta had been placed in absolute, unrestricted command. When the American Ambassador, toward the close of the long bombardment, appealed to President Madero to remove some federal batteries, the fire from which threatened the foreign quarter of Mexico City, President Madero replied that he had nothing to do with the military dispositions, and referred the Ambassador to General Huerta, who promptly acceded to the request. On another occasion, later in the bombardment, when Madero insisted that the federal artillery should use explosive shells against the Citadel, General Huerta did not hesitate to take it upon himself to countermand the President's suggestions to Colonel Navarrete, the federal chief of artillery. Afterwards General Navarrete admitted in a speech at a military banquet that his federal artillery "could have reduced the Citadel in short order had this really been desired."

Whether General Huerta could have won or not, is beside the issue, since he did not win and since the final turn of events plainly revealed that his heart had not been in the fight and that he had only been waiting for a favorable moment to turn against Madero. Before General Blanquet with his supposed relief column was allowed to enter the city, General Huerta had a private conference with Blanquet. This conference sealed Madero's doom. Later, after Blanquet's forces had been admitted to the Palace, on Huerta's assurances to the President that Blanquet was loyal to the government, it was agreed between the two generals that Blanquet should make sure of the person of the President, while Huerta would personally capture the President's brother, Gustavo, with whom he was to dine that day. The plot was carried out to the letter.

When Huerta put Gustavo Madero under arrest, still sitting at the table where Huerta was his guest, Huerta sought to palliate his action by claiming that Gustavo Madero had tried to poison him by putting "knock-out" drops into Huerta's after-dinner brandy. At the same time Huerta claimed that President Madero had tried to have him assassinated, on the day before, by leading Huerta to a window in the Palace, which an instant afterward was shattered by a rifle bullet from outside.

Neither of the two prisoners ever had a chance to defend themselves against these trumped up charges, for Gustavo Madero on the night following his arrest was shot to death by a squad of soldiers in the garden of the Citadel, and President Madero met a similar fate a few nights afterward. General Huerta, who by this time had got himself officially recognized as President, gave out an official statement from the Palace pretending that Gustavo Madero had lost his life while attempting to escape, and that his brother, the President, had been accidentally shot by some of his own friends who were trying to rescue him from his guard.

Nobody in Mexico, or out of it, ever believed this official version. Yet the murder of the two Maderos, and of Vice-President Pino Suarez, as well as the subsequent killing of other prisoners, like Governor Abraham Gonzalez of Chihuahua, or General Hernandez, the chief of the rurales, was condoned by many in Mexico on the ground that these men, if allowed to remain alive, were bound to make serious trouble for the new government. It was generally hoped, at the same time, even by those who condemned these murders as barbarous, that General Huerta might still prove himself a wise and able ruler, no matter how cruel.

These fond hopes were changed to gloomy foreboding only a few weeks after Huerta's assumption of the presidency, when he was seen to surround himself with notorious grafters and boodlers, of all kinds, and when he was seen to fall into Madero's old error of extending the "glad hand" to notorious rebels and bandits like Orozco, Cheche Campos, Tuerto Morales and Salgado.

Victoriano Huerta, whether he be considered as a general or as a president, can be expressed in one word. He is an Indian.

Huerta himself proudly says that he is a pure-blooded Oaxaca Indian. His friends claim for him that he has the virtues of an Indian, - courage, patience, endurance and dignified reserve. His enemies, on the other hand, profess to see in him some of the vices of Indian blood, - such as fondness for fire-water, fondness for gambling, treachery and blood lust.

From what I have seen of General Huerta, in the field, in private life, and as a President, I would say that he combines in himself both the virtues and the faults of his race. In battle I have seen him expose himself with a courage worthy of the best Indian traditions; nor have I ever heard it intimated by anyone that he was a coward. One of his strong points as a commander was that he was a man of few words. On the other hand his own soldiers at the front dreaded him as a stern and cruel leader; and some of the things that were done to his prisoners-of-war at the front were enough to curdle anyone's blood.

That Huerta is addicted to strong drink and often takes too much, is too well known in Mexico to admit of discussion. I have seen him repeatedly under the influence of drink. Many of his most serious mistakes, since he became President, have been committed under the influence of brandy. One of those was the appointment of his reputed relative, Enrique Cepeda, a notorious drunkard and degenerate, to the important office of Governor of the Federal District, - a post of power which Cepeda abused by murdering General Gabriel Hernandez, the late Commander-in-Chief of the rurales in Mexico, then a helpless prisoner in Belem jail.

It was during a moment of conviviality, likewise, that General Huerta once revealed his true sentiments toward the United States and our people. This was during a banquet given in his honor at Mexico City on the eve of his departure for the campaign in Chihuahua last year. On this occasion an Englishman, who had long been on terms of intimacy with Huerta, asked the General what he would do if northern Mexico should secede to the United States and the Americans should take a hand in the fray. This question aroused General Huerta to the following extemporary speech:

"I an not afraid of the Gringoes. Why should I be? No good Mexican need be afraid of the Gringoes. If it had not been for the treachery of President Santa Ana, who sold himself to the United States in 1847, we should have beaten the Yankees then, as we surely shall beat them the next time. Let them cross the Rio Bravo! We will send them back with bloody heads.

"We Mexicans need not be afraid of any foreign nation. Did we not beat the Spaniards? Did we not also beat the French, and the Austrians, and the Belgians, and all the other foreign adventurers who came with Maximilian? In the same way we would have beaten the Gringoes, had we had a fair chance at them. The Texans, who beat Santa Ana at San Jacinto, you must know, were not Gringoes but brother Mexicans, of whom we have reason to be proud.

"To my mind there are only two real nations in the world, besides our old Aztec nation. Those nations are England and Japan.

"All the others cannot properly be called nations, least of all, the United States, which is a mere hodge-podge of other nations. One of these days England and Japan and Mexico will get together, and after that there will be an end to the United States."

* * * * * * *

GENERAL FELIX DIAZ

By Edwin Emerson

Brigadier General Felix Diaz will be the next President of Mexico, provided he is allowed to live. He is bound to be elected in the next Mexican national elections inasmuch as no other candidate has been permitted to run against him. His claims to election are based entirely upon the fact that he is the nephew of ex-President Porfirio Diaz. As he himself expressed it to me: "I am a Portifista, first and last."

Felix Diaz, by the time Mexico's next elections come around will have passed his 47th birthday. Compared to our people of the North he appears a small, dark man with a tendency to plumpness, but in Mexico his type is very common. After the manner of Mexican military men he wears his black hair quite short with black mustaches slightly curled up at the ends. His eyes are brown, with a steady determined expression, and his teeth, when he shows them, appear white and regular. Like most Mexicans of Indian descent he rejoices in small hands and feet.

General Diaz's habitual attitude and manner is that of a man who takes himself very seriously. He seldom, if ever, smiles. His intimate friends say that he have never been heard to laugh since he has grown into manhood.

An old French gentleman in Mexico City, who knew Napoleon III, and who knows Felix Diaz well, tells me that General Diaz bears a striking resemblance to Louis Napoleon in the early fifties. Many Mexicans profess to see no less striking a resemblance between Felix Diaz and his uncle Porfirio, when the latter was in his forties. In fact, it is claimed by many Mexicans that Felix is one of several natural sons of General Porfirio Diaz. This legend, which appears to be apocryphal, rather flatters the nephew's vanity, it is said. At all events, he has never gone out of his way to put a stop to the ugly story.

In this, as in so many other respects, there is another obvious analogy between Felix Diaz and Napoleon III. Louis Napoleon, it will be recalled, never seriously discountenanced the Napoleonic legend that he was an illegitimate son of Hertense of Holland and his uncle, Napoleon Bonaparte.

There are further analogies. Both men, from their childhood, were imbued with definite notions of coming into power, some day or other, and both men, as soon as they had reached manhood plotted and schemed to seize the reins of government at the first opportunity that offered. Both men failed in their first attempt, but thanks to steady perseverance and the inheritance of a great name, succeeded in their final coups d'etat. Both men, furthermore, had the astuteness and good sense to appeal not only to the military passions of the army but to the greed of money and lust for power of the upper crust of society, and big business men, without whose cooperation no modern government can well prevail.

Felix Diaz's detracters in Mexico like to carry the analogy between him and Louis Napoleon even farther. Thus they point out that neither of the two men actually inherited any of the greater qualities of their illustrious uncles, that they both owed their temporary power purely to anti-republican acts of despotism and to the connivance of unscrupulous financiers, and that both used their power to plunge their countries into unnecessary warfare and bloodshed.

The following is from an anonymous popular broadside against Felix Diaz, which was pasted up on the street corners of Mexico City, one night recently, only to be torn down by the police next morning:

THE NEPHEW.

"Fellow Citizens: You all know the uncle. By this token you will also know the nephew.

"By inevitable laws of heredity, and of atavism, the nephew must be cruel and bloodthirsty, though otherwise he has none of the great qualities of the uncle.

"We hear nothing from the press. Nothing is said in Congress. Nobody dares speak his thoughts in a loud voice. But in dark corners, in alley-ways, behind closed doors, in whispers, everybody is talking about The Murder. We mean the murder of our constitutional president, Francisco I. Madero. Nobody has any doubt as to who was the instigator of this black crime.

"What a black shame that a country, professing to be Christian and civilized like ours, should proceed to elect for its president an assassin, a promoter of mutinies, of treason, a corrupter of our soldiers.

"Yes, we all want peace, we want tranquillity, we want to forget our rancors and our hatreds. But how can we hope for reconciliation, when the pretender to the throne is an assassin, who is backed up in his black deeds by the army?

"And this is what they call a free presidential election!

"Felix Diaz, the only candidate we are permitted to vote for, presents himself as our only salvation. The truth is that he is the cornerstone of all our monstrous edifice of disgrace. He is the apple of discord between our warring brethren, The menace of our liberties.

"They talk of reform. In reality they mean to restore a scion of our late discredited dynasty.

"Like the uncle, so the nephew.

"Like Porfirio, so Felix. He bears no love for liberty nor justice--only hate. He does not mean to educate our people in democratic ideas. He, on the contrary, he means to plant in our soil such poisonous growths as servility, hypocrisy, abject subjection. Already we are breathing the noisesome miasma of his ambitions.

"Listen to the whispers of the people!

"Should Felix Diaz die today, tomorrow all the newspapers, all the orators, all the people, would be crying from the housetops, what now is murmured only from ear to ear. They would brand him in letters of shame as the Murderer of Madero. But so long as Felix Diaz lives, be prepared. O Mexicans, to learn anew from the shameless nephew the bloody lessons first taught us by the uncle!"

Thanks to the zealous efforts of the police this significant manifesto has become a great rarity in Mexico, as rare as the original manifesto of the military revolution issued by Diaz and Huerta on the day after the fall of Madero, almost all the copies of which were mutilated and destroyed by the enraged populace.

From the above it must not be judged that Felix Diaz in his personal intercourse with men makes a sinister impression. Quite the contrary.

The first time I ever caught a personal glimpse of him was some eight years ago at a diplomatic reception given by his uncle, President Diaz, at the National Palace. Somebody pointed out a brilliantly uniformed young Mexican officer to me, telling me to take note of him as the chosen successor of Porfirio Diaz. My friend explained at the same time that this young man was Don Felix, the nephew of the President, and Chief of the President's military staff. When I asked my friend why the President's son, Don Porfirito, did not have as good or even a better chance, my companion shrugged his shoulders and said: "Evidently you have not met Don Porfirito." "Any way", he added, "They say that Felix is the elder brother of Porfirito--on the left side of the house, you understand."

After such a description I naturally took a good look at the young Chief of Staff. From his erect carriage, and bold fearless glance I judged, quite superficially of course, that he might, very likely, have the same stuff in him as a soldier and possible future ruler, as his warlike old uncle.

The last time I saw General Felix Diaz was at the opening of his recent presidential campaign, when he had betaken himself to the safe refuge of the Hacienda de Cristo, near Atzcapetzalco, some fifteen miles northwest of Mexico City. Here I found him in an inner chamber of the main building of the old ranch, serving for an antechamber, some forty or fifty men, mostly politicians, office seekers or old army comrades, were lounging about in small whispering groups, whiling away the time with cigarettes and occasional sips of brandy.

Outside of the big ante-room, in the corridors, were more men of an evidently humbler class, some of whom were the servants and orderlies of those inside, while the others, so I was told, were lesser job hunters.

In another, smaller room, adjoining the main sala, were a number of ladies, apparently engaged in the pleasant pastime of a merienda, the Mexican equivalent for an afternoon tea.

The whole scene, in its old Spanish setting, suggested the loves of audiencia of solo old Castilian grandee, as described by Le Sage in the immortal pages of "Gil Blas." After I had waited my turn, General Diaz received me alone and in a very matter of fact way immediately got down to the business of expressing his views for publication. Though Felix Diaz understands English well, he makes it a point, like his illustrious uncle, only to speak Spanish when talking for publication. Here are some of the things he said:

> "My attitude at present is necessarily one of expectancy. I am aware, of course, that my main hope for success lies in my relationship and identification with General Diaz.
> "Yes, I am an out and out Porfirista at heart, and I am glad that my countrymen, on emerging from the shadow of their late errors hasten to give their adherence to me, as a means of expressing through me their feeling toward my uncle.
> "It is true that the governmental methods of General Diaz were strictly his own, since they were based on historic events and personal achievements which were so conspicuously identified with him, that anyone, without his personal prestige who would seek to copy them would only court complete utter failure. Any new man, trying to follow in my uncle's footsteps, would be bound to find himself lacking the heroic reputation of the old leader, who drew his sword in a hundred battles to save the independence of our nation. He would lack the profound love and reverence of all these grizzly veterans who accompanied him in his many wars. So, too, he would not have behind him that blind faith with which our people confided their welfare to their old trusted leader. Lastly, he would lack the profound admiration and respect with which

foreign nations now love to honor our absent Chief
Magistrate as one of the greatest statesmen that the
19th century produced."

General Felix Diaz then went on to say how he meant to follow in
the footsteps of his uncle by adopting the same attitude of governmental
encouragement toward foreign capitalists, investors and colonists in
Mexico, most particularly toward Americans. Should there be another
influx of American and foreign capital, said General Diaz, he meant to
complete and carry on some of the great governmental measures of his
uncle, such as the perfecting of means of communication--railroads,
highways, bridges, waterways, and telegraph lines--and the
construction and improvement of harbor facilities. The main thing, he
recognized, was to put Mexico once more on a sound financial basis.
This, he added, could only be accomplished by thoroughgoing, drastic
measures of pacification.

With this end in view, General Diaz declared, he meant to build up
and strengthen the army and rural constabulary forces of the
government, a task in which he expected to be materially aided by the
assistance of his comrades-in-arms and recent fellow plotters, Generals
Huerta, Blanquet and Mondragon.

On such subjects as the needs of better public education, better
election laws, better prisons, reform institutions, hospitals and public
asylums, as well as any betterment of the present hard lot of the
common soldiers in Mexico, I was not able to elicit anything definite
from Senor Diaz. After considerable questioning he did commit himself,
though, to the following important utterance on the land problem, so
acute in Mexico at present.

> "I believe in a more equitable taxation of land
> in our country, and I mean to do all I can to help
> bring about this reform. I hold that our great
> land-holders should be made to pay taxes on their
> unimproved land, to the end that they will be
> impelled to dispose of their lands to smaller
> land-holders, who, in turn, will improve this land
> and pay taxes on it. Thus the government will not

only derive increased revenues, but some of our
arid wastes of land will be made to bloom, and some
of the present land hunger of the poorer country
folk will be satisfied."

It is such a far cry from words to deeds, especially in Mexico,
that a better way of gauging the good intentions and capacity for
government of Felix Diaz is to judge him from his past performances
and career, as a nephew, citizen, soldier, politician, governor and
rebel.

Felix Diaz, Jr., was born in the City of Oaxaca, near the Isthmus
of Tehuantepeo, in 1867, the eldest son of Brigadier General Felix Diaz
and Dona Josefa Prieto. When he was still a boy his father who had
distinguished himself in the war against the French, was cruelly
tortured to death on the Isthmus of Tehuantepeo by the natives of that
region in one of their many revolutions against the rule of his uncle,
Porfirio Diaz. In revenge for this Porfirio Diaz tried to exterminate most
of the male population on the Isthmus, so that there are many more
women there now than men.

From his early boyhood young Felix was destined for a military
career and was reared accordingly. In 1883 he entered the Military
Academy of Chapultepec, graduating in 1889 with a commission as
Second Lieutenant of Engineers. His first military service was with the
famous Geographical Commission of the army, which drew up the
Mexican General Staff's big military map of Veracruz and some adjoining
States. While working on this map he was promoted successively to First
Lieutenant and Captain. In 1898 he was ordered to the General Staff at
the Capital and served for a while as Chief of Staff ad interim in the
Presidential Palace. During the same year Felix Diaz married Isabel
Alcolea, the daughter of Don Leandre Alcolea, a Deputy of Veracruz.
On the expiration of his father-in-law's term in Congress, Felix Diaz,
now a Major, received a furlough from the army to run for his
father-in-law's vacant seat in Congress, to which he was duly elected
and reelected. His growing importance in politics was now come to be
viewed with suspicion by his uncle, President Porfirio Diaz, who

relieved him from his congressional duties and sent him off as a Consul General to Chile. This was in 1902, and came as an immediate consequence to the publication of an article in a Veracruz newspaper, in which Felix Diaz was extolled as the likeliest presidential successor to Don Porfirio.

After three years in South America, followed by a short trip through Europe, Felix Diaz was allowed to return and was reinstated in the army with the rank of Lieutenant Colonel. By way of keeping the young man under his eye President Diaz appointed him chief of his personal military staff. Within two years he was promoted to a Colonelcy and was made Inspector General of Police at the Capital. During his administration of this post, so it is said, Colonel Diaz achieved an unenviable distinction for ruthless severity and many police barbarities that never were allowed to be discussed in the open. Nevertheless he was kept in his post by his uncle until 1910, the crowning year of Don Porfirio's presidency, when suspicion once more fell upon Colonel Diaz because of his known presidential aspirations. At the same time he had furnished his political enemies, Ministers Limantour and Corral, with a powerful weapon against himself because of his growing financial and business enterprises, carried on as an important side issue to his administration of the metropolitan police. Consequently President Diaz suddenly deprived his nephew of his police command and sent him out of the country on a trip through the United States. Others say that the immediate cause of his falling out with his uncle was an unpleasant social scandal leading to a personal quarrel and fisticuff encounter between himself and Vice President Ramon Corral.

In 1911, when the Madero revolution had already spread to all parts of Mexico, Felix Diaz was recalled by his old uncle, in a forlorn hope that the young man might be able to come to the front as the saviour of Mexico. He was promoted to the command of a brigade, and at the head of his command was ordered down to Oaxaca, the native State of the Diaz family, to quell the growing rebellion there. All eyes were turned upon the young soldier as the possible salvation of Mexico, since this was the first time in his military career that he had been suffered to lead troops in the field; but, unfortunately for himself, he was unable to cut his way through to Oaxaca until the revolution in the south had already gained such headway that his pretended military governorship of that State proved another fiasco. By the time he attempted to assume command there his uncle had already given up the fight and was on his way to Europe.

During the interim presidency of Francisco Leon de la Barra, General Felix Diaz, after resigning his governorship of Oaxaca, which had never been generally recognized by the people of that State, strove to regain political control there by running once more for the governorship of his native State. Francisco Madero found it easy to spike Felix Diaz's guns by putting up Don Benito Juarez, Jr., the son of the old Indian president, who likewise hailed from Oaxaca, as a candidate against him. When it came to a vote in Oaxaca, General Felix Diaz was buried under an overwhelming avalanche of adverse votes. In the language of our own politicians he never had "a look in."

After this humiliating defeat General Felix Diaz resigned from military service and ostensibly retired to private life and the pursuit of his business affairs.

For more than a year little was heard of him until one day his countrymen were reminded of his existence by newspaper notices of a rather startling interview with Don Felix Diaz, published in a New York newspaper, in which Don Felix boldly denounced President Madero as a fool and a weakling, at the same time expressing his sympathy with the revolutionary aims of Pascual Orozco and Emiliano Zapata. Immediately after this Don Felix disappeared from Mexico City. Henceforth, whenever he was heard of in Mexico, it was in connection with alleged plots and conspiracies against the existing government. His name, together with those of Orozco and Zapata, became a rallying cry for the enemies of Madero.

Early in October of 1912, Don Felix Diaz suddenly appeared in the port of Veracruz, accompanied by his wife and family for a pretended visit to his brother-in-law, Leandro Alcolea, Jr., a prominent lawyer in Veracruz. There he was visited by many Mexican military officers, known to be disaffected toward the government, most prominent among when was Colonel Jose Diaz Ordaz. Madero's government immediately put him under police surveillance, but before any definite steps were undertaken Felix Diaz managed to get away during a fiesta by hiding under the seat of an automobile filled with children. He gained the railroad, at a wayside station, some distance out of Veracruz City, and traveling in a third-class car, disguised as a peon, reached Orizaba, where he was harbored by Colonel Diaz Ordas, then in command of the Twenty-First Battalion of Infantry, stationed there.

One week later, on October 16th, Colonel Ordaz obtained command of a special troop train, on the pretense that he was about to engage in active operations against General Aguilar, leader of a band of military insurgents near Orizaba. On this troop train, together with the soldiers and officers of the Twenty-First Battalion, Ordaz and Diaz steamed down to the port of Veracruz, entering that city at early dawn.

The rest is history. After marching to the regular military barracks, without having attracted any undue notice, the two rebel leaders succeeded in pursuading the other soldiers and officers quartered there to join in their mutiny. Thereupon they occupied the Commandansia, Police Headquarters, Municipal Palace, and Custom House. This done, printed placards were immediately posted all over the city in which Felix Diaz called upon the people of Veracruz to join his cause, promising them all manner of reform, better public order, justice and peace. The proclamation closed with these words: "Long live General Diaz! Long live the New Government! Long live the noble people of Veracruz!"

Soon a crowd of people gathered on the main plaza and were there addressed from the balcony of the military barracks by General Diaz.

The noise was such that he could barely make himself heard. All he was able to say on this occasion was: "Noble people of Veracruz! We must have peace and the army must be respected. Down with Francisco Madero and the robber Francisco Villa! Three cheers for peace and order! Long live the army!"

Though the city of Verz Cruz had thus easily fallen into the hands of Felix Diaz, his revolution was doomed to collapse because he failed to win over to his cause either the garrison of the harbor fort and prison of San Juan de Ullea or the commanders of the two little Mexican men-of-war that lay under the guns of that fort. The reason why Felix Diaz failed to win over these important elements, so it is understood, was because he did not have enough bribe money, since the steamer from New York that was to bring him additional funds arrived more than forty-eight hours after its scheduled time.

This was also the reason, so it is said, why the rebels failed in their attempts to induce Generals Beltran and Blanquet, of the regular army, who were sent against them from the Capital, to join hands with them. At all events General Beltran brought his loyal vanguard by train to Veracruz, and after a mere pretense of a fight in which the gunboats in the harbor took part by a long range bombardment of fifteen minutes, General Diaz surrendered to an officer of the loyal 18th Battalion, the advance skirmishers of which were the first to reach the plaza.

After his surrender and imprisonment in the Castle of San Juan de Ulloa, General Felix Diaz was man enough to take all the responsibility and blame for the attempted revolution, as well as for its failure, upon himself. Thereby he saved the lives of the twenty or more commissioned officers among the mutineers, who were involved in his plot. Felix Diaz himself, together with three of the military comrades, who openly confessed their guilt, were court-martialed and sentenced to death. Owing to General Diaz's previous resignation from the service, however, the sentence was set aside by President Madero and he was allowed to escape with his life. Diaz's fellow conspirators also were spared on the ground that they had been misled by him.

All were held as prisoners in the Castle of San Juan de Ullea, but there were so many rumors that Felix Diaz was to be done away with that President Madero presently ordered him to be removed from Veracruz to Mexico City.

The moment it became known that Felix Diaz had been saved from death and that he had been allowed to join the other political prisoners confined in the penitentiary at the Capital, his friends and sympathizers in Mexico City began to plot for his release.

The relatives and friends of Major General Bernardo Reyes, confined in the military prison on similar charges of sedition, because of his previous attempt at a military revolution in the north, naturally became invloved in these plots, which presently crystallized into a wide-spread military conspiracy for the overthrow of the Madero Government, under the leadership of General Manuel Mondragon.

This officer, apart from motives of friendship with General Reyes and Felix Diaz, had strong reasons of his own for plotting the downfall of President Madero, since the latter had ordered serious charges of dishonesty and fraud to be formulated against General Mondragon because of Mondragon's purchases of defective ordnance and artillery ammunition for the government, in his capacity as Chief Ordnance Officer under the presidency of Porfirio Diaz.

Together with General Mondragon and his son, as well as the son of General Bernardo Reyes, there were involved in the plot General Manuel M. Velasquez, stationed at Jalapa, Veracruz, who attended to the financing of the revolution through agents abroad; General Mariano Ruiz, who contributed $20,000 to the cause, besides opening his house in Tacubaya to the conspirators: his brother, General Gregorio Ruiz, and Colonel Anaya; Lieut. Colonels Gabriel Aguillon and Catalino Cruz in charge of the artillery barracks in Mexico City; Majors Terea and Zosaya, commanding cavalry squadrons under Col. Anaya in the outskirts of the city; Lieut. Gerardo Covarrubias, of the Military Academy of Chapultepec; together with all the military instructors and cadets of the Military College of Tlalpan, as well as a number of politicians and civilians, such as Cecilio Ocen, the proprietor of the Hotel Majestic, in the City of Mexico, Victor Velasquez, and Jose Mondragon, brothers of the above named generals, Licenciado Vera and Messrs. Duhart, Martin, Gutierrez, Ponado, with several other more or less prominent men.

The active participation of the above named persons was afterward openly revealed by Victor Jose Velasquez, one of the original conspirators. Many others, after the success of the revolution, claimed to have been in the plot, but most of these are regarded in Mexico as "ex-post facto" conspirators anxious for seats on the triumphal "band wagon."

There is a story which is very generally believed in Mexico, that General Huerta was invited into the conspiracy, giving his word of honor that he would not reveal its secrets to Madero. General Huerta, however, it is told, had a disagreement with General Mondragon over the question who was to succeed Madero in the presidency, General Huerta demanding the presidential office on his own behalf, as a reward for his promised treason, while Mondragon stuck fast to his imprisoned friend, General Felix Diaz, for president.

Thus it happened, so some of General Mondragon's friends now say, that General Huerta, having fallen out with the conspirators, chose the other alternative of standing by President Madero, until such time when he could make more advantageous terms with General Blanquet, the next highest commander in Mexico, who had been left out of the conspiracy because of his previous stand against Felix Diaz at Veracruz.

How the plot succeeded is sufficiently well known. During the
night and early morning of February 9th, the conspirators, after
cutting all the important telephone connections, proceeded in various
columns, some of which were provided with light batteries of artillery,
first to the liberation of their captive friends, General Reyes and Diaz,
in the Penitentiary and Military Prison, and next to armed assaults
upon the National Palace and the Citadel near the central market of the
city.

The assault on the Palace failed because General Lauro Villar, the
Commandant of the Palace, walking in citizen's dress to his office in the
early morning of February 9th, caught sight of a detachment of the
Tlalpan cadets, dragging a machine gun with them, and thus was
enabled to give the alarm and to have his men in readiness. Thus it
happened that General Reyes, so far from having the Palace betrayed
into his hands, as had been arranged, was received by an unexpected
machine gun fire and fell mortally wounded together with many of his
men and a great number of innocent people, who always fill the main
plaza of Mexico City in the early hours of the morning.

Meanwhile Generals Mondragon and Felix Diaz, marching by a
roundabout way through the more deserted streets of the city,
succeeded in reaching the Citadel and Arsenal, nearly a mile away from
the palace, where they were admitted by General Rafael Davila, after a
few point blank discharges of artillery against the Citadel, one of which
killed General Villarreal, the Commandant of the Citadel.

From a military point of view the capture of the Citadel was a
master stroke, since the building is not only a fortress in itself and so
situated that it completely dominates all approaches, but contained
besides a large arsenal of artillery, machine guns, small arms and
ammunition--more than could ever be used by the small body of men
who now manned its defenses. By seizing such nearby points as the tall
Y. M. C. A. building, and the big Balom prison whose convicts were
liberated and incorporated into the files of the revolutionists,

Mondragon and Diaz gained control of all the populous quarter of the city surrounding these points, as well as of the main market, thus making sure of ample provisions and recruits from the slums.

What a master stroke this capture of the Citadel was is proved by the fact that the government forces, throughout the ten days of street fighting that followed, never were able to dislodge the rebels from that strong vantage point. It is true that Colonel Navarrete, the chief of the government artillery forces, under General Huerta, afterward confessed that he was not permitted by his chief to reduce the Citadel in the proper way by an effective bombardment from the surrounding heights of the city, but the fact remains that several desperate attempts were made to storm the Citadel, all of which failed.

Finding that the small government forces that still stood by Madero were either unable or unwilling to force the reduction of the Citadel, and finding moreover that the foreign diplomats, under the leadership of the American Ambassador, had joined the hue and cry against the Constitutional Government, Madero's most trusted generals, Victoriano Huerta and Aureliano Blanquet, after previous secret communications between Blanquet and Diaz, suddenly "flopped" and made Madero their prisoner.

Felix Diaz has been generally credited in Mexico with being the master mind, who not only planned and executed the seizure of the Citadel, but who also first suggested and planned the stroke at the Palace by which Madero was made a prisoner. By the subsequent revolutions of Victor Jose Velasquez, one of the arch-conspirators, it has been made clear though, that General Mondragon was the man who, from the first, laid all the plans for an early capture of the Citadel, and he, too, was the man who laid the first plans for the ultimate betrayal of President Madero.

Felix Diaz's gratitude to General Mondragon has been shown not only by Mondragon's present appointment to the Ministry of War, which was insisted upon by Diaz, but also by General Diaz's solomn promise to continue Mondragon in his administration of the War Department after Huerta shall have given way to Diaz.

Whether Felix Diaz was the master mind who planned and caused the secret murder of his political enemies, Francisco Madero, Gustavo Madero and Pino Suarez, or whether these men were done to death by secret orders of Generals Huerta and Blanquet, is still a meeted question in Mexico and may never be cleared up.

President Huerta still insists on his original version that Gustavo Madero was shot while trying to escape, and that Francisco Madero together with Pino Suarez had the misfortune to be hit by stray bullets during a midnight attempt to deliver them from their guards while on the way from one prison to another. While insisting on this official explanation General Huerta has not hesitated to reward the officer who had charge of the prisoners, on the night when they were killed, by promoting him from a captain to a major.

General Blanquet wisely says nothing.

Felix Diaz, while saying nothing, gently raises his eyebrows at General Huerta's official version and shrugs his shoulders.

Only one incriminating circumstance has been allowed to leak out so far. This is the fact that a man, known to be a close friend of General Diaz, hired from a public garage one of the two automobiles in which Francisco Madero and Pino Suarez were taken from the Palace on the night of their murder. When this man sent for the machine, on the night of their murder, he expressly stipulated that he would pay the full purchase price in case he should decide not to return the machine next morning. At the same time he said that he might decide to keep its chauffeur in his regular employment.

The machine was returned to the public garage on the following morning, riddled with bullets and with one of its cushions soaked with blood. The chauffeur never returned to his old employer.

In reply to inquiries concerning him it was announced that he had been detained as a witness in the tragedy. Nobody was allowed to get at him. The next that was heard of the chauffeur was that he had been shipped to Europe with money enough to keep him out of Mexico for the rest of his life.

General Diaz's friends in Mexico, however, insist that the general had nothing whatever to do with the murder of Madero. They say it was a private act of vengeance on the part of a few men who were burning to avenge the death of General Bernardo Reyes and of certain officers and cadets, such as Colonet Vasconcelos and the son of General Blanquet, for instance, who were killed during the fighting at the Palace. Nobody denies, though, that these vengeful men were the intimate friends of Felix Diaz.

Even though it is claimed on behalf of General Diaz that he is innocent of this foul crime, neither he nor any of his friends have gone so far as to pretend that he has ever expressed the slightest regret for Madero's death.

Whether Felix Diaz becomes President of Mexico or not, it is safe to say that the remaining members of the Madero family and their many thousand friends in Mexico will always look upon him as the man most directly responsible for the Madero murder.

COPY OF PRIVATE LETTER FROM MEXICAN OFFICIAL

When I arrived in Mexico in January, public opinion had decidedly turned against Madero. It seems that he was a dreamer, partly a [one word illegible] partly a visionary, thoroughly qualified to act the role of the prophet or apostle to move the rabble and lower classes towards a millennium, constantly offered, and never to be attained. Our washer-woman, had become an enemy of Madero, because she claimed him faithless to his promise, in as much as she had to work as hard as ever, instead of becoming rich at once under his Government, as he had promised, (such, she said) during the revolution. So that, in January not even artisans and workmen, composing the lower strata of the middle class, were Maderoists any longer, and it was only the very lowest of the lower class that retained faith in their so called apostle.

Of course the leading classes had seen through Madero long before. His power as an agitator, (very great because even of the vagueness of his speeches, which as they were indefinite, did not clash with anybody's ideas, and on the contrary seemed to fall in with everybody's ideals and wishes) was not associated with any constructive or organizing faculties, and his government which had brought only anarchy, ruin and disorder to Mexico, was since July 1912 or thereabouts, actually falling to pieces, and Mexico was a picture of the bad place, where, according to theologians the worst picture of torment endured is that "there is no hope left". Madero had a most powerful enemy, he could never get rid of his self, his destructive faculty was incredible, and peace, order, authority, Congress, municipalities, police, Army, everything that constitutes the machinery of Government was so thoroughly disorganized and prostituted by him, that the conveyance spread far and wide, that with Madero, we had to repeat Dante's "lassciate egui speranza"; "abandon hope all ye who live under Madero's rule". And it was evident that the Army was the only force that could put an end to Madero's inferno.

It was as if the house was burning; one had to throw on it in torrents all the available water to put out the flames, even if that very same torrent would cause some damage to the furniture and decoration. The house had to be saved, quickly, or it would perish with all that it contained. And history repeats itself; to create order out of Madero's political chaos and anarchy, a military Government was accepted; but I must say that it was not absolutely military; because really the old men in the Senate, (and a leader among them, a banker, Don Sebastian Camache, nearly 90 years old, one of the wealthy and most respected men in the City of Mexico) were the true organs of public opinion, and the moral force of the movement of which the Army was an instrument. Mr. Camache walked to the palace with a group of his friends, and urged on Madero the necessity of his resignation, pointing out to him the fiasco of his administration, the national ruin brought about by his ambition, the exhausted treasury, the impossibility of negotiating a loan while he misgoverned the country, and all the shame and falseness of his dream democracy. These old men could have been the heroes of the day; their efforts were unsuccessful with Madero, who would not resign, but the moral blow they struck at Madero was more powerful to bring about his downfall, than all the shots and shell fired from the Citadel.

The end came with all its horrors and regretable bloodshed; but in spite of them I consider that Mexico has been saved from the desolation and annihilation. National Credit has been reestablished, we are arming ourselves with heart and soul to put down the rebels on the North, and the bandits who are bent on maintaining disorder, and for the first time we have the hope of securing peace within a few months. Of course our greatest difficulty is in the Northern frontier States where the sympathies of the people along the American Border are always on the side of those who fight against any Government in Mexico, and who would like to create trouble at all times in Mexico and between Mexico and the United States.

We need to have the work of pacification advance in order to hold a presidential election in October, and we are working for it earnestly and in the work of reconstruction Europe has given us their moral aid and pecuniary assistance. Our loan for $160,000,000 has been negotiated in Paris and our provisional Government has been recognized by all the great European powers. This has caused a great current of sympathy towards the old countries across the Atlantic and even a Commercial boycott of American goods has been talked about; but the Mexican Government is doing all it can to prevent Anti-American demonstrations, which is right, because it is to the true interest of both nations to further trade and friendly relations between them. I regret to say that the invasion of our Ports by American Men-of-War, absolutely needless (as facts have proved it to be) and the non-recognition of our Provisional Government at Washington seem to indicate that friendly sentiments on this side are not fully reciprocated by our next door neighbors. You will easily understand that this is very harmful to our Government in its work of pacification to the commerce of both the U.S. and Mexico; and to the furtherance of a friendly intercourse between our two Countries, which so many Americans and Mexicans have truly at heart. Our provisional Government has been constituted by Congress according to the Mexican Constitution, has been recognized by the World at large, and is endeavoring to carry out the work of reconstruction, so much needed after Madero's revolution. It is a mystery to me why the powers that be at Washington do not recognize it. People here claim that the idea is to create difficulties to the new Government in its work of pacification and to prevent the negotiating of the loan in order that the financial ruin inherited from Madero may be the ruin and the end of the present administration. Of course I do not believe any such Machiavellian plan and do my utmost to convince all Mexicans I come in contact with that they are mistaken, yet the motives and the actions of your Government towards Mexico is surrounded with mystery and seems difficult to explain. I hope that they may soon recognize our Government and withdraw their Men-of-War, in order that we, who, are bent on maintaining friendly sentiments between the two countries and furthering our Commerce with the U. S., may be able to evoke the susceptibilities of my countrymen, justly aroused by the contrast of the action of the American Government and that of other Countries with whom we have diplomatic relations.

Fortunately, as I said before, the loan has been secured and you will see now how rapidly the work of pacification will prosper until we return to peace and prosperity interrupted by Madero and other border revolutionists.

Please consider this letter confidential and do not couple my name with it if you happen to quote any part of it to strangers.

I am studying my country now, so badly changed, from four years ago, and firmly believe that the Madero episode of ruin and desolation has come to an end and that the present Government, although far from the ideal of us who do not like to see soldiers as Chief Magistrate of the Republic, to put things in order. Later on we may gradually work towards better things; but now we want peace, and military force is needed to attain it.

I am working today in the reorganization of the finances of the State of Tavecala[?]. I congratulate you on the victory of your friends the Democrats. I suppose their presence in W-- will make life there more pleasant and I wish I could help, even with a small little grain of sand to their popularity throughout all the Americas. I hope they will give us a chance by and by, sympathizing in our troubles and helping us as a big brother, even as other countries, situated far beyond the seas are doing now, lending their moral aid to us Mexicans in our efforts to bring back peace and prosperity to our native land."

*   *   *   *   *   *

- End -

INDEX

Clapham, Charles R. (Master
Mechanic, Mazapil Copper Co.)
  shot during Carransista attack,
    25, 164

Coahuila & Zacatecas Railway
  in disfavor of General Lopez,
    164-165

Compania Maderera de la Sierra,
  lumber camps of robbed, 76

Concepcion del Oro, Zacatecas
  fighting between Carransistas
    and Federals in, 24-26;
  mining camps in, 55;
  capture of, 164-165

Contreras, Calixto
  commands rebels in Durango,
    75;
  making headquarters near Dur-
    ango City, 76, 78;
  encamped at San Ignacio Ranch,
    81;
  concentrating in Cararia and
    Canatlan, 89

Contreras, Tirso
  killed in Sombrerete, 137

Cordova
  Mexican Railway Company has
    engines in, 40

Corral, Ramon (Vice President
under Diaz)
  quarrels with Felix Diaz, 197

Corrales, Carlos
  killed by bandits, 137

Crawford, James
  is stabbed near Panuco, 108-
    109;
  attempts made on father's life,
    110

Criterio
  publishes article on Americans
    in Durango, 82-83

Cruz, Catalino
  role of in plot against
    Madero, 201

Cuatlan
  Zapatistas in, 39

Cuba
  disagrees with Wilson's
    policy, 148

Cueller, General Garcia (Governor of Federal District)
  meets with Delbert Huff, 123

Cuernavaca
  Huerta's campaign in, 175

Culiacan
  Maderistas in, 39

Diaz, Felix, 46
  is most honest politician, 36;
  Wilson visits to seek a truce,
    65;
  meets with General Huerta at
    American Embassy, 65-66;
  role in overthrow of Madero,
    132-133;
  money to be used in Madero
    overthrow by, 144;
  release of demanded, 144;
  takes possession of arsenal,
    146;
  Wilson's feelings toward, 147;
  plans new Mexican government,
    154, 173;
  captures Veracruz port, 184;
  biographical sketch of by
    Edwin Emerson, 190-206

Diaz, Porfirio, 46
  Limantour loses patience with,
    14;
  revolutionists demand resigna-
    tion of, 16-17;
  de la Barra doubts resignation
    of, 19;
  popularity & cabinet decisions
    of discussed, 20-22;

226

United States (cont'd)
  citizens of in Mexico, 42;
  army of training Mexican sol-
    diers, 44;
  intervention by could be
    dangerous, 45;
  northern Mexican states want
    annexation to, 45-46;
  must come to aid of Mexico, 47;
  feelings in Mexico toward cit-
    izens of, 54;
  attitude of lax regarding con-
    ditions in Mexico, 57;
  should not listed to ill-
    informed people concerning
    Mexico, 62-63, 69;
  is strong in Mexico, 66;
  fear of results of intervention
    by, 72;
  loan of arms by refused, 82-83

Uruchurtu, Deputy Manuel R.
  bill introduced by ignored, 30

Valles
  rebels take money from, 112;
  attack on expected, 118

Vallesteres, Colonel Luis
  takes over penitentiary, 158

Velardena
  captured by rebels, 93

Velasquez, Manuel M., 201

Velasquez, Victor Jose
  reveals names of co-conspira-
    tors in plot against Madero,
    202
  involvement in conspiracy, 204

Vera Cruz (Mexican gunboat)
  prisoners taken aboard, 106

Vera Cruz
  elections pending in, 32;
  foreigners not protected in,
    108;
  jurisdiction of Military Com-
    mander in, 120-121;
  ammunition moved from, 146;
  port of captured by Felix Diaz,
    184;

Felix Diaz's campaign in, 199-
  200

Vera-Estanol, Jorge (head of
Evolutionist Party) 21
  on Madero's list of people to
    be shot, 61;
  to be Minister of Education,
    154

Victoria
  surrounded by revolutionists,
    108;
  protection of, 120

Victoria, General Guadelupe, 171

Villa, Francisco
  rebels awaiting arrival of,
    89;
  Huerta fabricates charges
    against, 181

Villar, General Lauro (Diaz
General in northern Mexico)
  caused assault on Palace to
    fail, 203

Vought, M.I.
  injured attempting to protect
    family, 118

Walker, H.
  letter by concerning murder of
    Madero, 60-63;
  letter by concerning bombard-
    ment of Mexico City, 64-67;
  discusses Wilson's valor and
    Barrett's ignorance, 68-73;
  letter by concerning Madero &
    Wilson, 74

Warfield, Lewis (President, Occidental Construction Company)
  view of Diaz' popularity and
    correspondence with Liman-
    tour, 20-23

Washington Conference (concerning reforms & peace in Mexico)
16-19

Whiffin, _____ (Associated Press
representative) 124